**EL** ESSENTIALS

—// ON //—

# Poverty
## *and*
# Learning

EL ESSENTIALS

— // ON // —

# Poverty
*and*
# Learning

Readings from
*Educational Leadership*

—•&————//————&•—

Edited by
Marge Scherer

ASCD

Alexandria, VA USA

**ASCD®**

1703 N. Beauregard St. • Alexandria, VA 223111714 USA
Phone: 800-933-2723 or 703-578-9600 • Fax: 703-575-5400
Website: www.ascd.org • E-mail: member@ascd.org
Author guidelines: www.ascd.org/write

Deborah S. Delisle, *Executive Director*, Robert D. Clouse, *Managing Director, Digital Content & Publications;* Stefani Roth, *Publisher;* Genny Ostertag, *Director, Content Acquisitions;* Julie Houtz, *Director, Book Editing & Production;* Julie Huggins, *Editorial Assistant;* Thomas Lytle, *Senior Graphic Designer;* Mike Kalyan, *Manager, Production Services;* Cynthia Stock, *Production Designer;* Andrea Wilson, *Senior Production Specialist*

***Educational Leadership* Staff**
Margaret M. Scherer, *Editor in Chief;* Deborah Perkins-Gough, *Senior Editor;* Kim Greene, *Senior Associate Editor;* Naomi Thiers, *Associate Editor;* Lucy Robertson, *Associate Editor;* Judi Connelly, *Associate Art Director*

PDF E-BOOK ISBN: 978-1-4166-2229-1   ASCD product #116064E4   n3/16
See Books in Print for other formats.
Quantity discounts: 10–49, 10%; 50+, 15%; 1,000+, special discounts (e-mail programteam@ascd.org or call 800-933-2723, ext. 5773, or 703-575-5773). For desk copies, go to www.ascd.org/deskcopy.

23 22 21 20 19 18 17 16          1 2 3 4 5 6 7 8 9 10 11 12

**EL** ESSENTIALS

—// ON //—

# Poverty
# *and*
# Learning

# Introduction

## The Poor—
## Not So Very Different, After All

> Let me tell you about the very poor. They are different from you and me. They do not possess what they need and they suffer early, and it does something to them, makes them hard where we are soft, and cynical where we are trustful, in a way that, unless you were born poor, it is very difficult to understand.

After reading Jonathan Kozol's evocative book, *Fire in the Ashes* (Broadway Books, 2012), the portraits of children growing up in abject poverty stayed with me. After a while, I found myself rewriting the famous F. Scott Fitzgerald quote (above) in which he crystalized his understanding of the very rich.[1] By substituting just a few words, I found I could create a myth about the poor, which, like Fitzgerald's characterization of the rich, rings true to some degree. The kids in Kozol's book who survived life in a hellhole tenement in New York City in the 1980s suffered some lasting scars that even later interventions and reversal of fortunes could not change. Those who did thrive did so because of their own inner strengths, and they often persisted as a result of the loving concern of the adults, especially teachers, who had reached out to them.

Although we all know that poverty changes the lives of children—and changes our lives, too—the polarized viewpoints of the day make us all eager to look for someone else—the government, philanthropists, charities and churches, the schools, or the poor themselves—to find the solutions. We may even believe that nothing can change.

In this compilation of articles about poverty and learning selected from past issues of *Educational Leadership*, our authors provide insights into the challenges that children who live in poverty face and the kind of solutions that are possible today.

Throughout the collection, the authors demythologize poverty as a culture and urge educators to see "students of poverty" as students who happen to be poor (Landsman, Gorski, Jensen). They look at the reasons for the existence and persistence of the uneven playing field (Rothstein, Kozol) and the solutions that can open up opportunities for students who deserve an equal chance (Potter, Neuman, Nisbett, McGill-Franzen and Allington, Parrett and Budge). Some of our authors help educators identify the students who may be part of the invisible poor—those who are homeless (Dill) and those whose frequent moves interrupt their schooling (Smith and colleagues). And all inspire us to try both little *and* big interventions that will make a difference (Nisbett, Tomlinson, Burke, and Naomi Thiers's interview with Salome Thomas-EL).

Throughout each article, authors express a sense of urgency, for poverty is not something that affects a small minority. More than 51 percent of children who attend our public schools live in poverty. As Steve Suitts recently noted at the ASCD Whole Child Symposium on poverty and education, "We've reached the juncture in our public schools where the education of low-income students is not simply a matter of equity and fairness. It's a matter of our national future.... If public education in this country fails, the nation fails, and that is the message we have to come to grips with."[2]

–Marge Scherer
Editor in Chief, *Educational Leadership*

# Endnotes

[1] Fitzgerald, F.S. (1926, January/February). The rich boy. *Redbook*. Retrieved from Gutenberg.net. au/fsf/THE-RICH-Boy.html.

[2] ASCD. (2015). Poverty and education. (A report on the spring 2015 Whole Child Symposium). Alexandria, VA: Author.

# Overcoming the Challenges of Poverty

Julie Landsman

*Here are 15 things educators can do to make our schools
and classrooms places where students thrive.*

Last year, when I was leading a staff development session with teachers at a high-poverty elementary school, a teacher described how one of her kindergarten students had drifted off to sleep at his seat—at 8:00 a.m. She had knelt down next to the child and began talking loudly in his ear, urging him to wake up. As if to ascertain that she'd done what was best for this boy, she turned to the rest of us and said, "We are a 'no excuses' school, right?"

A fellow teacher who also lived in the part of Minneapolis where this school was located and knew the students well, asked, "Did you know Samuel has been homeless for a while now? Last night, there was a party at the place where he stays. He couldn't go to bed until four in the morning."

I couldn't help but think that if the "no excuses" philosophy a school follows interferes with basic human compassion for high-needs kids, the staff needs to rethink how they are doing things. Maybe they could set up a couple of cots for homeless students in the office to give them an hour or two of sleep; this would yield more participation than shouting at children as they struggle to stay awake.

This isn't the first time I've heard of adults viewing low-income children as "the problem" rather than trying to understand their lives. In a radio interview I heard, a teenage girl in New Orleans after Hurricane Katrina told her interviewer that she thought many people viewed poor families like hers as criminals. Crying, she described how it felt when city officials blamed her family for the lack of food and shelter they experienced after the hurricane.

## A Forgotten Duty?

Sometimes it seems that we do not believe it's our duty to provide basic needs and an education for all children in the United States, no matter where they grow up. For instance, in some schools I know of, when a student cannot pay for a reduced-price meal, the lunch is dumped into the trash in front of the entire school, humiliating that child.

The attitudes of policymakers also reflect a shift toward teaching students in differing ways depending on their economic status. Teachers often hear that poor kids come from violent, chaotic homes and that only regimented curriculums will allow them to succeed. Although wealthier children are taught through a variety of approaches that emphasize developing the whole child, the emphasis for low-income children is often on developing obedience.

At the same time, many rural, urban, and suburban schools serving low-income students challenge such prescriptive teaching. They quietly provide, intellectually and materially, for high-poverty students. For instance, they create programs that arrange transportation for students to theaters, concerts, and museums. Because Saturday and Sunday are two days of the week many poor children go hungry, some schools send kids home for the weekend with backpacks of food.

They create a welcoming environment where even the poorest parents feel comfortable.

Teachers and administrators at these schools offer challenging instruction while simultaneously addressing basic needs. This is a tricky balancing act that requires dedication, self-reflection, and reexamining what works—or doesn't. Here, gathered from schools that succeed with students living in poverty, are suggestions for how to manage that balancing act.

# What Teachers Can Do

## Make Time for Extras

Can you create times for students to make up schoolwork, work on a project for history class, or just enjoy music and art? It doesn't have to be every day. Teachers in a building might coordinate to set times before and after classes during which a child with an unstable home life can use a computer or read in silence—and when teachers can give guidance and build trust.

In one middle school where I worked, we let students spend their lunch hours with us, providing chess and checkers. It's amazing how much information young men and women will share over a game board, from tasks they're having trouble accomplishing to worries about food over the weekend. What we learned from these times helped us create programs that met students' greatest needs.

## Tell Students to Ask for Help

Spell out that you expect learners to come talk with you about a low test score, a comment on a paper, or their needs for resources. Some students simply don't know the expectations regarding behavior, work, and interaction with their teacher. One teacher in a suburban high school assumed her students had access to the Internet and assigned work on the basis of that assumption. When she found out that many students had no Internet at home, she organized time after classes for students to work on school computers—and transportation home—giving careful instructions about what she wanted from their time online.

Cut deals with students who don't have essential supplies by providing those supplies while, at the same time, pushing these kids to work hard on their assignments. A homeless girl may have lost a pencil in the trudge around the city finding a place for the night or left her homework in the office of a shelter. A boy may not be able to get his work done by the due date because he has no quiet place to concentrate. By keeping a supply of pencils, paper, and notebooks handy and adjusting due dates for individual students, you can make sure students know you're willing to modify conditions but you expect work to be done.

## Use Visuals to Help Organize Assignments

Students whose lives are chaotic need to be reminded of exactly what work is due and when. Calendars and charts are visual cues that help kids organize time and tasks together, especially if you refer to them often. Write different tasks and events connected to each assignment— outline due date, media center day, or first draft due—on the calendar squares. A calendar both reminds students of the day of the week and creates a visual map to future tasks.

## Imagine Their Obstacles—and See Their Strengths

If you grew up with economic security, remind yourself that you might not understand the things adults and children in families with barely enough for the basics have to do just to survive—and the obstacles they face. Some schools expect parents to get to parent conferences in the evening, which can involve a bus ride, babysitting expense, or taking time off from the late shift. To illuminate what such expectations involve, one school's social worker surveyed parents and teachers to see how many owned cars. Every teacher and teacher's aide owned a car, but only 40 parents—in a school with 500 students—did.

Find ways to accommodate such realities. For instance, I worked as a visiting poet in a school where one-third of the students were homeless. We made sure each kid had two copies of the poems they wrote, one to leave at school and one to take to their parents, to keep their writing from getting lost in transit.

When high-poverty schools hire people from the surrounding neighborhood who are acquainted with the poverty there, these people can be experts regarding students' situations. Connect with these staff members; ask their advice on how to affirm and provide for particular children. Jared, a young adult hall monitor at a school where I taught writing, brought into my class a poetry book by rapper Tupac Shakur. I read some of those poems with my students. Soon Jared was visiting my poetry sessions during breaks from his work, helping students with their writing and homework.

Understanding students' obstacles should help you give them credit for their amazing resilience and delight in learning. Low-income children are often described in terms of what they *don't* have or *cannot* do. Reframe your thinking to recognize the strength it takes for a child who had to find a couch to sleep on last night to simply make it in the school door.

## Listen

In our rush to create silent classrooms and push test preparation, we lose sight of the complexity of children's lives, and we lose our delight in knowing how they, feel, reason, joke, or concoct ideas. In just 10 minutes, you can encourage students to write from a prompt like "I am from _____" or "I used to_____, but now I _____." Read their pieces to a small group or to the entire class. Elementary teachers often have a daily circle time and even in secondary school, you can pull the chairs into a circle at the end of class and ask students about their plans for the rest of the day or a neighborhood event.

This listening is an important part of your job. Listening means slowing down or stopping, even for a minute as a student lingers by your desk. It means having music playing as you work in your classroom in the morning and nodding to a student who comes in early. If you let that student relax there most mornings, he might make it a habit to talk with you before each day begins.

## Don't Tolerate Teasing

By establishing clear classroom guidelines, including no teasing about clothes or possessions and talking with students about what these guidelines mean, you'll establish a climate of safety. Effective guidelines state positive behaviors, such as: Be Physically Considerate, Be Verbally Considerate, or Try New Things. Talk about what concepts like *consideration* mean; for instance, showing verbal consideration includes not taunting or hurting anyone's feelings. When you spend time up front working on behaviors, you save time the rest of the year. Classes become communities, and discipline problems diminish.

## Connect Curriculum to Students' Interests

When possible, connect the content you're teaching to things students are fascinated with, like a song or video they keep talking about or the pollution in their neighborhood. By tapping into learners' concerns, you can develop bridges to literature, science, or math. You might engage students in projects connected to community issues or problems, like cleaning up a playground or advocating for a bus for summer programs. Students can write letters to the editor, ask scientists to come in and talk about pollution, or find journalists who will talk to the class about issues in their city. Such actions give low-income students a sense of agency and possibility. You might also infuse their families' traditions and talents into classwork. Financially poor students often come from families rich in culture.

## Speak Out

Advocate for impoverished children by speaking up about which students are tracked into general courses versus gifted programs or advanced classes. Insist on the giftedness of some of your poorer students. Some schools have programs that parallel advanced classes yet don't require applicants to demonstrate academic skills that they may not have going in—but could develop. These demanding courses both challenge and support low-income students.

Other schools have opened up advanced placement or International Baccalaureate classes to anyone who wants to try them. Suggest similar programs and push for changes like providing bilingual conferences for parents who don't speak English. You may get push back from those who want no deviation from the status quo. Be willing to be unpopular for your advocacy.

## Find Allies

It's hard to do this work in isolation. Forge a supportive network that keeps you going as you strive to make a difference for students and push for academic equity—through a book group, inquiry team, or lunchtime discussion on issues related to education and poverty. You'll have someone to call when you're trying to anticipate how your suggestions will go over at the next faculty meeting—and someone to talk with about how it went. There are more teachers willing to advocate for kids than is often apparent.

# What Administrators Can Do

Principals and superintendents can do much to support both struggling students and committed teachers. Think in terms of getting resources to the neediest schools and students.

## Develop a Trusting Relationship with Teachers

Can teachers talk with you about an idea or solution they have for addressing the needs of poorer students? One of the most successful urban principals I ever worked with asked teachers to come to him often with a problem combined with a suggested solution.

Standing up for overworked teachers builds trust. When the district tries to mandate more requirements or protocols in March or to add a new test, voice your concern for the load this might put on teachers, many of whom may be already providing for students materially. When you have a devoted staff, make sure they know you'll challenge those who would add more burdens.

## Spend Time in Classrooms

Observe not to evaluate, but to see how teachers do what they do successfully. Administrators, counselors, social workers, and even superintendents can be remarkable supporters for teachers by coming to classrooms—to work with students on a project, play piano for them, or just talk to them. When done in cooperation with teachers, such encounters add a great deal to a school's collaborative climate.

## Give Teachers a Picture of Students' Realities

Through tapping the insights of social workers and district demographic services, and through family surveys, find out what household income and resources are like in your area and what resources students probably do or don't have at home. Share with your faculty facts like the income ranges of your families or the absence of grocery stores or libraries in their neighborhoods—details that clarify what it means to be poor.[1]

This information will help teachers avoid assumptions about what students have in their homes and appreciate the resilience of youth from high-poverty families who get to school each day filled with hope and energy.

## Advocate for High-Quality Classes

Be aware of how tracking works in your school or district. Are poor students getting slotted into classes for low-skilled students early in their lives? Advocate for low-income kids to receive gifted education services.

Get more teachers into the neediest classrooms. A principal who states publicly that having five classes each containing 45 students is unacceptable—and that he or she will work to change these conditions—wins teachers' trust.

## Offer After-school Programs and Services

Work with teachers to find groups like the YMCA to provide volunteers for your school, so students have supervision and stimulation—including physical activities, art, and academic activities—more hours in the day. Local groups, businesses, and cultural venues will often contribute if approached by the principal or superintendent (see Figure 1.1). Consider providing wraparound services for your low-income students, such as access to medical and mental health professionals.

## Communicate Commitment

Make clear that as an administrator, you're in this for the long haul and will work on long-term solutions to inequity for children in your district. It is important that your entire staff knows you will persist in getting the services and programs your building needs.

# Toward Vibrant Classrooms

These are just a few ways educators can ensure students aren't marginalized by poverty—without making students feel they are a "problem." Each school district will need to explore what might work in its unique situation. But my hope is that no school ever becomes a place where sleepy children are yelled at or where teachers lose our human compassion. Let's create vibrant classrooms that tap into the brilliance of each child.

---

**Figure 1.1: Sources of Grants for Projects and Materials**

**RGK Foundation** awards grants for projects in K–12 education (math, science, reading, and teacher development) and after-school enrichment programs. The foundation is interested in programs that attract female and minority students into STEM.

**National Geographic Education Foundation** provides professional development and education materials connected to geography education.

**American Honda Foundation** supports youth and scientific education projects, including those that offer unique approaches to teaching youth in minority and underserved communities.

**Dollar General Literacy Foundation** funds programs for youth and adult literacy, school library relief, and preparation for the GED. Dollar General Grant Programs support nonprofits in U.S. states in which company stores are located.

**The ING Foundation** awards grants to nonprofits working in education, particularly physical education and for programs addressing child obesity.

**Teaching Tolerance** makes grants of $500 to $2,500 for projects designed to reduce prejudice, improve intergroup relations in schools, and support professional development in these areas.

---

## Endnote

[1] Many documentaries and public television programs (such as A Place at the Table, Viva la Causa, and Why Poverty) show what life is like for families living in poverty—for example, the realities of doubling up with relatives or taking two bus rides to get groceries.

---

**Julie Landsman** (julie@jlandsman.com) is a consultant on equitable education. She is the author of many books on education, including *A White Teacher Talks About Race* (R & L Education, 2005), and is the coeditor with Paul Gorski of *The Poverty and Education Reader* (Stylus, 2014).

Originally published in the June 2014 issue of *Educational Leadership*, 71: pp. 16–21.

# 2

# The Myth of the Culture of Poverty

Paul Gorski

*Presuming that people with lower incomes are culturally different from those with higher incomes often results in stereotyping.*

As the students file out of Janet's classroom, I sit in the back corner, scribbling a few final notes. Defeat in her eyes, Janet drops into a seat next to me with a sigh.

"I *love* these kids," she declares, as if trying to convince me. "I adore them. But my hope is fading."

"Why's that?" I ask, stuffing my notes into a folder.

"They're smart. I know they're smart, but . . ."

And then the deficit floodgates open: "They don't care about school. They're unmotivated. And their parents—I'm lucky if two or three of them show up for conferences. No wonder the kids are unprepared to learn."

At Janet's invitation, I spent dozens of hours in her classroom, meeting her students, observing her teaching, helping her navigate the complexities of an urban midwestern elementary classroom with a growing percentage of students in poverty. I observed powerful moments of teaching and learning, caring and support. And I witnessed moments of internal conflict in Janet, when what she wanted to believe about her students collided with her prejudices.

Like most educators, Janet is determined to create an environment in which each student reaches his or her full potential. And like many of us, despite overflowing with good intentions, Janet has bought into the most common and dangerous myths about poverty.

Chief among these is the "culture of poverty" myth—the idea that poor people share more or less monolithic and predictable beliefs, values, and behaviors. For educators like Janet to be the best teachers they can be for all students, they need to challenge this myth and reach a deeper understanding of class and poverty.

## Roots of the Culture of Poverty Concept

Oscar Lewis coined the term *culture of poverty* in his 1961 book *The Children of Sanchez*. Lewis based his thesis on his ethnographic studies of small Mexican communities. His studies uncovered approximately 50 attributes shared within these communities: frequent violence, a lack of a sense of history, a neglect of planning for the future, and so on. Despite studying very small communities, Lewis extrapolated his findings to suggest a universal culture of poverty. More than 45 years later, the premise of the culture of poverty paradigm remains the same: that people in poverty share a consistent and observable "culture."

Lewis ignited a debate about the nature of poverty that continues today. But just as important—especially in the age of data-driven decision making—he inspired a flood of research. Researchers around the world tested the culture of poverty concept empirically (see Billings, 1974; Carmon, 1985; Jones & Luo, 1999). Others analyzed the overall body of evidence regarding the culture of poverty paradigm (see Abell & Lyon, 1979; Ortiz & Briggs, 2003; Rodman, 1977).

These studies raise a variety of questions and come to a variety of conclusions about poverty. But on this they all agree: *There is no such thing as a culture of poverty.* Differences in values and behaviors among poor people are just as great as those between poor and wealthy people.

In actuality, the culture of poverty concept is constructed from a collection of smaller stereotypes which, however false, seem to have crept into mainstream thinking as unquestioned fact. Let's look at some examples.

**MYTH:** Poor people are unmotivated and have weak work ethics.

**The Reality:** Poor people do not have weaker work ethics or lower levels of motivation than wealthier people (Iversen & Farber, 1996; Wilson, 1997). Although poor people are often stereotyped as lazy, 83 percent of children from low-income families have at least one employed parent; close to 60 percent have at least one parent who works full-time and year-round (National Center for Children in Poverty, 2004). In fact, the severe shortage of living-wage jobs means that many poor adults must work two, three, or four jobs. According to the Economic Policy Institute (2002), poor working adults spend more hours working each week than their wealthier counterparts.

**MYTH:** Poor parents are uninvolved in their children's learning, largely because they do not value education.

**The Reality:** Low-income parents hold the same attitudes about education that wealthy parents do (Compton-Lilly, 2003; Lareau & Horvat, 1999; Leichter, 1978). Low-income parents are less likely to attend school functions or volunteer in their children's classrooms (National Center for Education Statistics, 2005)—not because they care less about education, but because they have less *access* to school involvement than their wealthier peers. They are more likely to work multiple jobs, to work evenings, to have jobs without paid leave, and to be unable to afford child care and public transportation. It might be said more accurately that schools that fail to take these considerations into account do not value the involvement of poor families as much as they value the involvement of other families.

**MYTH:** Poor people are linguistically deficient.

**The Reality:** All people, regardless of the languages and language varieties they speak, use a full continuum of language registers (Bomer, Dworin, May, & Semingson, 2008). What's more, linguists have known for decades that all language varieties are highly structured with complex grammatical rules (Gee, 2004; Hess, 1974; Miller, Cho, & Bracey, 2005). What often are assumed to be *deficient* varieties of English— Appalachian varieties, perhaps, or what some refer to as Black English Vernacular—are no less sophisticated than so-called "standard English."

**MYTH:** Poor people tend to abuse drugs and alcohol.

**The Reality:** Poor people are no more likely than their wealthier counterparts to abuse alcohol or drugs. Although drug sales are more visible in poor neighborhoods, drug use is equally distributed across poor, middle class, and wealthy communities (Saxe, Kadushin, Tighe, Rindskopf, & Beveridge, 2001). Chen, Sheth, Krejci, and Wallace (2003) found that alcohol consumption is *significantly higher* among upper middle class white high school students than among poor black high school students. Their finding supports a history of research showing that alcohol abuse is far more prevalent among wealthy people than among poor people (Diala, Muntaner, & Walrath, 2004; Galea, Ahern, Tracy, & Vlahov, 2007). In other words, considering alcohol and illicit drugs together, wealthy people are more likely than poor people to be substance abusers.

## The Culture of Classism

The myth of a "culture of poverty" distracts us from a dangerous culture that does exist—the culture of classism. This culture continues to harden in our schools today. It leads the most well intentioned of us, like my friend Janet, into low expectations for low-income students.

It makes teachers fear their most powerless pupils. And, worst of all, it diverts attention from what people in poverty *do* have in common: inequitable access to basic human rights.

The most destructive tool of the culture of classism is deficit theory. In education, we often talk about the deficit perspective—defining students by their weaknesses rather than their strengths. Deficit theory takes this attitude a step further, suggesting that poor people are poor because of their own moral and intellectual deficiencies (Collins, 1988). Deficit theorists use two strategies for propagating this world view: (1) drawing on well-established stereotypes, and (2) ignoring systemic conditions, such as inequitable access to high-quality schooling, that support the cycle of poverty.

The implications of deficit theory reach far beyond individual bias. If we convince ourselves that poverty results not from gross inequities (in which we might be complicit) but from poor people's own deficiencies, we are much less likely to support authentic antipoverty policy and programs. Further, if we believe, however wrongly, that poor people don't value education, then we dodge any responsibility to redress the gross education inequities with which they contend. This application of deficit theory establishes the idea of what Gans (1995) calls the *undeserving poor*—a segment of our society that simply does not deserve a fair shake.

If the goal of deficit theory is to justify a system that privileges economically advantaged students at the expense of working-class and poor students, then it appears to be working marvelously. In our determination to "fix" the mythical culture of poor students, we ignore the ways in which our society cheats them out of opportunities that their wealthier peers take for granted. We ignore the fact that poor people suffer disproportionately the effects of nearly every major social ill. They lack access to health care, living-wage jobs, safe and affordable housing, clean air and water, and so on (Books, 2004)—conditions that limit their abilities to achieve to their full potential.

Perhaps most of us, as educators, feel powerless to address these bigger issues. But the question is this: Are we willing, at the very least, to tackle the classism in our own schools and classrooms?

This classism is plentiful and well documented (Kozol, 1992). For example, compared with their wealthier peers, poor students are more likely to attend schools that have less funding (Carey, 2005); lower teacher salaries (Karoly, 2001); more limited computer and Internet access (Gorski, 2003); larger class sizes; higher student-to-teacher ratios; a less-rigorous curriculum; and fewer experienced teachers (Barton, 2004). The National Commission on Teaching and America's Future (2004) also found that low-income schools were more likely to suffer from cockroach or rat infestation, dirty or inoperative student bathrooms, large numbers of teacher vacancies and substitute teachers, more teachers who are not licensed in their subject areas, insufficient or outdated classroom materials, and inadequate or nonexistent learning facilities, such as science labs.

Here in Minnesota, several school districts offer universal half-day kindergarten but allow those families that can afford to do so to pay for full-day services. Our poor students scarcely make it out of early childhood without paying the price for our culture of classism. Deficit theory requires us to ignore these inequities—or worse, to see them as normal and justified.

What does this mean? Regardless of how much students in poverty value education, they must overcome tremendous inequities to learn. Perhaps the greatest myth of all is the one that dubs education the "great equalizer." Without considerable change, it cannot be anything of the sort.

## What Can We Do?

The socioeconomic opportunity gap can be eliminated only when we stop trying to "fix" poor students and start addressing the ways in which our schools perpetuate classism. This includes destroying the inequities listed above as well as abolishing such practices as tracking and ability grouping, segregational redistricting, and the privatization of public schools. We must demand the best possible education for all students—higher-order pedagogies, innovative learning materials, and holistic teaching and learning. But first, we must demand basic human rights for all people: adequate housing and health care, living-wage jobs, and so on.

Of course, we ought not tell students who suffer today that, if they can wait for this education revolution, everything will fall into place. So as we prepare ourselves for bigger changes, we must

- Educate ourselves about class and poverty.
- Reject deficit theory and help students and colleagues unlearn misperceptions about poverty.
- Make school involvement accessible to all families.
- Follow Janet's lead, inviting colleagues to observe our teaching for signs of class bias.
- Continue reaching out to low-income families even when they appear unresponsive (and without assuming, if they are unresponsive, that we know why).
- Respond when colleagues stereotype poor students or parents.
- Never assume that all students have equitable access to such learning resources as computers and the Internet, and never assign work requiring this access without providing in-school time to complete it.
- Ensure that learning materials do not stereotype poor people.
- Fight to keep low-income students from being assigned unjustly to special education or low academic tracks.
- Make curriculum relevant to poor students, drawing on and validating their experiences and intelligences.
- Teach about issues related to class and poverty—including consumer culture, the dissolution of labor unions, and environmental injustice—and about movements for class equity.

- Teach about the antipoverty work of Martin Luther King Jr., Helen Keller, the Black Panthers, César Chávez, and other U.S. icons—and about why this dimension of their legacies has been erased from our national consciousness.
- Fight to ensure that school meal programs offer healthy options.
- Examine proposed corporate-school partnerships, rejecting those that require the adoption of specific curriculums or pedagogies.

Most important, we must consider how our own class biases affect our interactions with and expectations of our students. And then we must ask ourselves, Where, in reality, does the deficit lie? Does it lie in poor people, the most disenfranchised people among us? Does it lie in the education system itself—in, as Jonathan Kozol says, the savage inequalities of our schools? Or does it lie in us—educators with unquestionably good intentions who too often fall to the temptation of the quick fix, the easily digestible framework that never requires us to consider how we comply with the culture of classism.

## References

Abell, T., & Lyon, L. (1979). Do the differences make a difference? An empirical evaluation of the culture of poverty in the United States. *American Anthropologist, 6*(3), 602–621.

Barton, P. E. (2004). Why does the gap persist? *Educational Leadership, 62*(3), 8–13.

Billings, D. (1974). Culture and poverty in Appalachia: A theoretical discussion and empirical analysis. *Social Forces, 53*(2), 315–323.

Bomer, R., Dworin, J. E.,May, L., & Semingson, P. (2008). Miseducating teachers about the poor: A critical analysis of Ruby Payne's claims about poverty. *Teachers College Record, 110*(11). Available: www.tcrecord.org/PrintContent. asp?ContentID=14591

Books, S. (2004). *Poverty and schooling in the U.S.: Contexts and consequences.* Mahway, NJ: Erlbaum.

Carey, K. (2005). *The funding gap 2004: Many states still shortchange low-income and minority students.* Washington, DC: Education Trust.

Carmon, N. (1985). Poverty and culture. *Sociological Perspectives, 28*(4), 403–418.

Chen, K., Sheth, A., Krejci, J., & Wallace, J. (2003, August). *Understanding differences in alcohol use among high school students in two different communities.* Paper presented at the annual meeting of the American Sociological Association, Atlanta, GA.

Collins, J. (1988). Language and class in minority education. *Anthropology and Education Quarterly, 19*(4), 299–326.

Compton-Lilly, C. (2003). *Reading families: The literate lives of urban children.* New York: Teachers College Press.

Diala, C. C., Muntaner, C., & Walrath, C. (2004). Gender, occupational, and socioeconomic correlates of alcohol and drug abuse among U.S. rural, metropolitan, and urban residents. *American Journal of Drug and Alcohol Abuse, 30*(2), 409–428.

Economic Policy Institute. (2002). *The state of working class America 2002–03.* Washington, DC: Author.

Galea, S., Ahern, J., Tracy, M., & Vlahov, D. (2007). Neighborhood income and income distribution and the use of cigarettes, alcohol, and marijuana. *American Journal of Preventive Medicine, 32*(6), 195–202.

Gans, H. J. (1995). *The war against the poor: The underclass and antipoverty policy.* New York: BasicBooks.

Gee, J. P. (2004). *Situated language and learning: A critique of traditional schooling.* New York: Routledge.

Gorski, P. C. (2003). Privilege and repression in the digital era: Rethinking the sociopolitics of the digital divide. *Race, Gender and Class, 10*(4), 145–76.

Hess, K. M. (1974). The nonstandard speakers in our schools: What should be done? *The Elementary School Journal, 74*(5), 280–290.

Iversen, R. R., & Farber, N. (1996). Transmission of family values, work, and welfare among poor urban black women. *Work and Occupations, 23*(4), 437–460.

Jones, R. K., & Luo, Y. (1999). The culture of poverty and African-American culture: An empirical assessment. *Sociological Perspectives, 42*(3), 439–458.

Karoly, L. A. (2001). Investing in the future: Reducing poverty through human capital investments. In S. Danzinger & R. Haveman (Eds.), *Understanding poverty* (pp. 314–356). New York: Russell Sage Foundation.

Kozol, J. (1992). *Savage inequalities: Children in America's schools.* New York: HarperCollins.

Lareau, A., & Horvat, E. (1999). Moments of social inclusion and exclusion: Race, class, and cultural capital in family-school relationships. *Sociology of Education, 72*, 37–53.

Leichter, H. J. (Ed.). (1978). *Families and communities as educators.* New York: Teachers College Press.

Lewis, O. (1961). *The children of Sanchez: Autobiography of a Mexican family.* New York: Random House.

Miller, P. J., Cho, G. E., & Bracey, J. R. (2005). Working-class children's experience through the prism of personal storytelling. *Human Development, 48*, 115–135.

National Center for Children in Poverty. (2004). *Parental employment in low-income families*. New York: Author.

National Center for Education Statistics. (2005). *Parent and family involvement in education: 2002–03*. Washington, DC: Author.

National Commission on Teaching and America's Future. (2004). *Fifty years after Brown v. Board of Education: A two-tiered education system*. Washington, DC: Author.

Ortiz, A. T., & Briggs, L. (2003). The culture of poverty, crack babies, and welfare cheats: The making of the "healthy white baby crisis." *Social Text, 21*(3), 39–57.

Rodman, R. (1977). Culture of poverty: The rise and fall of a concept. *Sociological Review, 25*(4), 867–876.

Saxe, L., Kadushin, C., Tighe, E., Rindskopf, D., & Beveridge, A. (2001). *National evaluation of the fighting back program: General population surveys, 1995–1999*. New York: City University of New York Graduate Center.

Wilson, W. J. (1997). *When work disappears*. New York: Random House.

**Paul Gorski** (gorski@edchange.org) is Assistant Professor in the Graduate School of Education, Hamline University, St. Paul, Minnesota, and the founder of EdChange (www.edchange.org).

Originally published in the April 2008 issue of *Educational Leadership, 65*(7): pp. 32–36.

# 3

# How Poverty Affects Classroom Engagement

Eric Jensen

*Students from low-income households are more likely
to struggle with engagement—for seven reasons.*

Poverty is an uncomfortable word. I'm often asked, "What should I expect from kids from low-income households?" Typically, teachers are unsure what to do differently.

Just as the phrase *middle class* tells us little about a person, the word *poverty* typically tells us little about the students we serve. We know, for example, that the poor and middle classes have many overlapping values, including valuing education and the importance of hard work (Gorski, 2008). But if poor people were exactly the same cognitively, socially, emotionally, and behaviorally as those from the middle class, then the exact same teaching provided to both middle-class students and students from poverty would bring the exact same results.

But it doesn't work that way. In one study of 81,000 students across the United States, the students not in Title I programs consistently reported higher levels of engagement than students who were eligible for free or reduced-price lunch (Yazzie-Mintz, 2007). Are children from poverty more likely to struggle with engagement in school?

The answer is yes. Seven differences between middle-class and low-income students show up at school. By understanding those differences and how to address them, teachers can help mitigate some of the negative effects of poverty.

But first, my most important suggestion is to get to know your students well. Without respect—and without taking time to connect with your students—these seven factors will mean little.

## Difference 1: Health and Nutrition

Overall, poor people are less likely to exercise, get proper diagnoses, receive appropriate and prompt medical attention, or be prescribed appropriate medications or interventions. A study by two prominent neuroscientists suggested that intelligence is linked to health (Gray & Thompson, 2004). The poor have more untreated ear infections and hearing loss issues (Menyuk, 1980); greater exposure to lead (Sargent et al., 1995); and a higher incidence of asthma (Gottlieb, Beiser, & O'Connor, 1995) than middle-class children. Each of these health-related factors can affect attention, reasoning, learning, and memory.

Nutrition plays a crucial role as well. Children who grow up in poor families are exposed to food with lower nutritional value. This can adversely affect them even in the womb (Antonow-Schlorke et al., 2011). Moreover, poor nutrition at breakfast affects gray matter mass in children's brains (Taki et al., 2010). Skipping breakfast is highly prevalent among urban minority youth, and it negatively affects students' academic achievement by adversely affecting cognition and raising absenteeism (Basch, 2011).

When students experience poor nutrition and diminished health practices, it's harder for them to listen, concentrate, and learn. Exposure to lead is correlated with poor working memory and weaker ability to link cause and effect. Kids with ear infections may have trouble with sound discrimination, making it tough to follow directions, do highly demanding auditory processing, and understand the teacher. This can hurt reading ability and other skills. Poor diets also affect behavior. Students can often appear listless (with low energy) or hyperactive (on a sugar "high").

## What You Can Do

Remember, the two primary foods for the brain are oxygen and glucose; oxygen reacts with glucose to produce energy for cell function. Schools can provide these at zero cost. Having students engage in slow stretching while taking slow deep breaths can increase their oxygenation. Yoga training has been shown to increase metabolic controls so children can better manage themselves.

Recess and physical education contribute to greater oxygen intake and better learning (Winter et al., 2007). Never withhold recess from students for a disciplinary issue; there are countless other ways to let them know they behaved inappropriately. Children need physical education programs at every level to perform well academically. In addition, the use of games, movement, and drama will trigger the release of glucose, stored in the body as glycogen. Proper glucose levels are associated with stronger memory and cognitive function. In short, physical activity will reduce some of the issues associated with poor nutrition and will build student health.

# Difference 2: Vocabulary

Children who grow up in low socioeconomic conditions typically have a smaller vocabulary than middle-class children do, which raises the risk for academic failure (Walker, Greenwood, Hart, & Carta, 1994). Children from low-income families hear, on average, 13 million words by age 4. In middle-class families, children hear about 26 million words during that same time period. In upper-income families, they hear a staggering 46 million words by age 4—three times as many as their lower-income counterparts (Hart & Risley, 1995). In fact, toddlers from middle- and upper-income families actually used more words in talking to their parents than low-SES mothers used in talking to their own children (Bracey, 2006). This language difference is not subtle; it's a mind-boggling, jaw-dropping cognitive chasm.

A child's vocabulary is part of the brain's tool kit for learning, memory, and cognition. Words help children represent, manipulate, and reframe information. Kids from low-income families are less likely to know the words a teacher uses in class or the words that appear in reading material. When children aren't familiar with words, they don't want to read, often tune out, or feel like school is not for them. Also, many students don't want to risk looking stupid (especially to their peers), so they won't participate in class.

## What You Can Do

Vocabulary building must form a key part of enrichment experiences for students, and teachers must be relentless about introducing and using new words. Include vocabulary building in engagement activities, such as by creating "trading card" activities, in which students write a vocabulary word on one side of a 3 × 5 card and a sentence using the word correctly on the other. Students can do a "class mixer" and test other students; they give the new word to their partner, and their partner has to use it in a sentence. Teachers can also draw cards from a bowl and ask the class to use the new word in a sentence.

Teachers can incorporate vocabulary practice into daily rituals. For example, the teacher posts a word for the day and when either the teacher or a student uses it—and another student is first to point it out—that student gets a simple privilege. Classroom teams or cooperative groups should present a word for the day to the whole class every day, with teachers reinforcing those words for days and weeks afterward.

# Difference 3: Effort

Uninformed teachers may think that poor children slouch, slump, and show little effort because they are—or their parents are—lazy. Yet research suggests that parents from poor families work as much as parents of middle- or upper-class families do (Economic Policy Institute, 2002). There's no "inherited laziness" passed down from parents.

One reason many students seem unmotivated is because of lack of hope and optimism. Low socioeconomic status and the accompanying financial hardships are correlated with depressive symptoms (Butterworth, Olesen, & Leach, 2012). Moreover, the passive "I give up" posture may actually be learned helplessness, shown for decades in the research as a symptom of a stress disorder and depression. Research from 60 high-poverty schools tells us that the primary factor in student motivation and achievement isn't the student's home environment; it's the school and the teacher (Irvin, Meece, Byun, Farmer, & Hutchins, 2011). Effort can be taught, and strong teachers do this every day.

Students who show little or no effort are simply giving you feedback. When you liked your teacher, you worked harder. When the learning got you excited, curious, and intrigued, you put out more effort. We've all seen how students will often work much harder in one class than in another. The feedback is about themselves—and about your class.

Take on the challenge. Invest in students who are not putting out effort. In a study of more than 1,800 children from poverty, school engagement was a key factor in whether the student stayed in school (Finn & Rock, 1997).

## What You Can Do

First, strengthen your relationships with students by revealing more of yourself and learning more about your students. Ask yourself, "What have I done to build relationships and respect? Do my students like me?"

Use more buy-in strategies, such as curiosity builders (a mystery box or bag); excitement and risk ("This idea's a bit crazy; let's make sure we have the number for the fire department, just in case"); and competition ("My last class accomplished _____; let's see what you can do!"). Make the learning more of the students' idea by offering a choice, and involve them more in decision making.

Second, teachers must make connections to students' worlds in ways that help them see a viable reason to play the academic game. Can you tie classroom learning to the real world? Use money, shopping, technology, and their family members to make the learning more relevant. Without clear links between the two, students often experience a demotivating disconnect between the school world and their home life. As a result, they give up.

Third, affirm effort every day in class. Most teachers don't keep track of their comments to students; maybe they should. When teachers give more positives than negatives (a 3:1 ratio is best), they optimize both learning and growth (Fredrickson & Losada, 2005). When affirmed, challenged, and encouraged, students work harder.

Fourth, set high goals and sell students on their chances to reach them. Get them to believe in the goals by showing them real-world success stories of adults who came from the same circumstances the students did and who achieved their goals.

Finally, provide daily feedback so students see that effort matters and that they can adjust it for even greater success. Affirm your students, and let them know how much good you see in them.

## Difference 4: Hope and the Growth Mind-Set

Hope is a powerful thing. Research suggests that lower socioeconomic status is often associated with viewing the future as containing more negative events than positive ones (Robb, Simon, & Wardle, 2009). Low or no expectancy ("helplessness") is also related to low socioeconomic status (Odéen et al., 2012). In short, being poor is associated with lowered expectations about future outcomes.

The student's attitude about learning (his or her mind-set) is also a moderately robust predictive factor (Blackwell, Trzesniewski, & Dweck, 2007). Taken together, hope—or the lack of hope—and mind-set—whether you believe that you're simply born smart or that you can grow in intelligence along the way—can be either significant assets or serious liabilities. If students think failure or low performance is likely, they'll probably not bother to try. Similarly, if they think they aren't smart enough and can't succeed, they'll probably not put out any effort.

### What You Can Do

Teacher and student beliefs about having a fixed amount of "smarts" that the student can't increase will influence engagement and learning. Teach students that their brains can change and grow, that they can even raise their IQs. Provide better-quality feedback (prompt, actionable, and task-specific).

Also, telling students that they have a limited amount of focusing power is likely to disengage many of them (Miller et al., 2012). There's an alternative to saying, "Don't feel bad that you didn't finish. It's late in the day, and we've all got brain drain." Instead, say, "Stick with this just a bit longer. You can do this! Your mind is a powerful force to help you reach your goals."

Don't use comforting phrases that imply that even though a student isn't good at something, he or she has "other" strengths (Cooper, 2012). Instead, focus on affirming and reinforcing effort. Guide students in making smarter strategy choices and cultivating a positive attitude.

## Difference 5: Cognition

Children from lower socioeconomic backgrounds often perform below those from higher socioeconomic backgrounds on tests of intelligence and academic achievement (Bradley & Corwyn, 2002). Commonly, low-SES children show cognitive problems, including short attention spans, high levels of distractibility, difficulty monitoring the quality of their work, and difficulty generating new solutions to problems (Alloway, Gathercole, Kirkwood, & Elliott, 2009). These issues can make school harder for children from impoverished backgrounds.

Many children who struggle cognitively either act out (exhibit problem behavior) or shut down (show learned helplessness). But cognitive capacity, as well as intelligence, is a teachable skill (Buschkuehl & Jaeggi, 2010).

If you're not teaching core cognitive skills, rethink your teaching methods. Students who struggle with reading, math, and following directions may have weak vocabulary, poor working memory, or poor processing skills. Studies show that high-performing teachers can overcome the problems of underperforming kids (Ferguson, 1998). Like effort, cognitive capacity is teachable.

## What You Can Do

Focus on the core academic skills that students need the most. Begin with the basics, such as how to organize, study, take notes, prioritize, and remember key ideas. Then teach problem-solving, processing, and working-memory skills.

Start small. Teach students immediate recall of words, then phrases, then whole sentences. This will help them remember the directions you give in class and will support them as they learn how to do mental computations. This will take tons of encouragement, positive feedback, and persistence. Later, you can use this foundation to build higher-level skills.

# Difference 6: Relationships

When children's early experiences are chaotic and one or both of the parents are absent, the developing brain often becomes insecure and stressed. Three-quarters of all children from poverty have a single-parent caregiver.

In homes of those from poverty, children commonly get twice as many reprimands as positive comments, compared with a 3:1 ratio of positives to negatives in middle-class homes (Risley & Hart, 2006). If caregivers are stressed about health care, housing, and food, they're more likely to be grumpy and less likely to offer positive comments to their kids.

The probability of dropping out and school failure increases as a function of the timing and length of time that children are exposed to relational adversity (Spilt, Hughes, Wu, & Kwok, 2012). Having only a single caregiver in the home—if the father is absent, for example—can create both instability and uncertainty because the children are missing a role model. Two caregivers offer the luxury of a backup—when one parent is at work, busy, or overly stressed, the other can provide for the children so there's always a stabilizing force present. Relationships can be challenging for children who lack role models and sufficient supports.

Low-income parents are often less able than middle-class parents to adjust their parenting to the demands of their higher-needs children (Paulussen-Hoogeboom, Stams, Hermanns, & Peetsma, 2007). For example, many parents don't know what to do with children who have attention deficit hyperactivity disorder (ADHD), who are oppositional, or who are dyslexic.

Disruptive home relationships often create mistrust in students. Adults have often failed them at home, and children may assume that the adults in school will fail them, too. Classroom misbehaviors are likely because many children simply do not have the at-home stability or repertoire of necessary social-emotional responses for school. Students are more likely to be impulsive, use inappropriate language, and act disrespectful—until you teach them more appropriate social and emotional responses.

## What You Can Do

Children with unstable home lives are particularly in need of strong, positive, caring adults. The more you care, the better the foundation for interventions. Learn every student's name. Ask about their family, their hobbies, and what's important to them. Stop telling students what to do and start teaching them how to do it.

For example, if you ask a high school student to dial down his or her energy for the next few minutes and the student responds with a smirk or wisecrack, simply ask him or her to stay a moment after class. Never embarrass the student in front of his or her peers. After class, first reaffirm your relationship with the student. Then demonstrate the behavior you wanted (show the student the appropriate facial expression and posture); say why it will be important as the student moves through school ("This will keep you out of trouble with other adults"); and indicate when a given response is appropriate and what it should look like ("When you think your teacher has overstepped his or her bounds, this is what you should say"). End by affirming common goals and interests ("We're both in this together. We can make this work—if we each do our part").

# Difference 7: Distress

Although small amounts of stress are healthy, acute and chronic stress—known as distress—is toxic. Children living in poverty experience greater chronic stress than do their more affluent counterparts. Low-income parents' chronic stress affects their kids through chronic activation of their children's immune systems, which taxes available resources and has long-reaching effects (Blair & Raver, 2012). Distress affects brain development, academic success, and social competence (Evans, Kim, Ting, Tesher, & Shannis, 2007). It also impairs behaviors; reduces attentional control (Liston, McEwen, & Casey, 2009); boosts impulsivity (Evans, 2003); and impairs working memory (Evans & Schamberg, 2009).

Distressed children typically exhibit one of two behaviors: angry "in your face" assertiveness or disconnected "leave me alone" passivity. To the uninformed, the student may appear to be either out of control, showing an attitude, or lazy. But those behaviors are actually symptoms of stress disorders—and distress influences many behaviors that influence engagement.

The more aggressive behaviors include talking back to the teacher, getting in the teacher's face, using inappropriate body language, and making inappropriate facial expressions. The more passive behaviors include failing to respond to questions or requests, exhibiting passivity, slumping or slouching, and disconnecting from peers or academic work.

## What You Can Do

Address the real issue—distress—and the symptoms will diminish over time. Begin by building stronger relationships with students; this helps alleviate student stress.

Reduce stress by embedding more classroom fun in academics. Provide temporary cognitive support—that is, help students get the extra glucose and oxygen they need—by having them engage in such sensory motor activities as the childhood game "head-toes-knees-shoulders," in which children touch different parts of their bodies in quick succession. Such actions can support behavioral regulation, which is so important for early academic success.

Next, don't try to exert more control over the student's life. This will only create continued issues with engagement. Instead, give students more control over their own daily lives at school. Encourage responsibility and leadership by offering choices, having students engage in projects, and supporting teamwork and classroom decision making. Having a sense of control is the fundamental element that helps diminish the effects of chronic and acute stress.

Finally, teach students ongoing coping skills so they can better deal with their stressors. For example, give them a simple, "If this, then that" strategy for solving problems using new skills. You can do this through telling stories about your own daily stressors, allowing students to brainstorm solutions, and then sharing the coping tools that worked for you and modeling how you addressed various challenges.

## Seeing Clearly

Remember, students in poverty are not broken or damaged. In fact, human brains adapt to experiences by making changes—and your students can change.

You can help them do so by understanding these seven differences and addressing these differences with purposeful teaching. Your school can join the ranks of the many high-performing Title I schools where students succeed every day.

## References

Alloway, T. P., Gathercole, S. E., Kirkwood, H., & Elliott, J. (2009). The cognitive and behavioral characteristics of children with low working memory. *Child Development, 80*(2), 606–621.

Antonow-Schlorke, I., Schwab, M., Cox, L. A., Lic, C., Stuchlika, K., Wittea, O. W., et al. (2011). Vulnerability of the fetal primate brain to moderate reduction in maternal global nutrient availability. *Proceedings of the National Academy of Sciences of the United States of America, 108*(7), 3011–3016.

Basch, C. E. (2011). Breakfast and the achievement gap among urban minority youth. *Journal of School Health, 81*(10), 635–640.

Blackwell, L. S., Trzesniewski, K. H., & Dweck, C. S. (2007). Implicit theories of intelligence predict achievement across an adolescent transition. *Child Development, 78*(1), 246–263.

Blair, C., & Raver, C. C. (2012). Child development in the context of adversity. *American Psychology, 67*(4), 309–318.

Bracey, G. W. (2006). Poverty's infernal mechanism. *Principal Leadership, 6*(6), 60.

Bradley, R. H., & Corwyn, R. F. (2002). Socioeconomic status and child development. *Annual Review of Psychology, 53*, 371–399.

Buschkuehl, M., & Jaeggi, S. M. (2010). Improving intelligence. *Swiss Medical Weekly, 140*, 266–272.

Butterworth, P., Olesen, S. C., & Leach, L. S. (2012). The role of hardship in the association between socio-economic position and depression. *Australia and New Zealand Journal of Psychiatry, 46*, 364–373.

Cooper, L. A. (2012, May/June). Do "consoling" messages hinder math achievement? *Harvard Education Letter, 28*(3).

Economic Policy Institute. (2002). *The state of working class America 2002–03.* Washington, DC: Author.

Evans, G. W. (2003). A multimethodological analysis of cumulative risk and allostatic load among rural children. *Developmental Psychology, 39*(5), 924–933.

Evans, G. W., Kim, P., Ting, A. H., Tesher, H. B., & Shannis, D. (2007). Cumulative risk, maternal responsiveness and allostatic load among young adolescents. *Developmental Psychology, 43*(2), 341–351.

Evans, G. W., & Schamberg, M. A. (2009, April 21). Childhood poverty, chronic stress, and adult working memory. *Proceedings of the National Academy of Sciences of the United States of America, 106*(13), 6545–6549.

Ferguson, R. (1998). *Evidence that schools can narrow the black-white test score gap.* Cambridge, MA: Malcolm Wiener Center for Social Policy.

Finn, J. D., & Rock, D. A. (1997). Academic success among students at risk for school failure. *Journal of Applied Psychology, 82*(2), 221–234.

Fredrickson, B. L., & Losada, M. F. (2005). Positive affect and the complex dynamics of human flourishing. *American Psychologist, 6*(7), 678–686

Gorski, P. (2008). The myth of the culture of poverty. *Educational Leadership, 65*(7), 32–36.

Gottlieb, D. J., Beiser, A. S., & O'Connor, G. T. (1995). Poverty, race, and medication use are correlates of asthma hospitalization rates. *American College of Chest Physicians, 108*(1), 28–35.

Gray, J. R., & Thompson, P. M. (2004). Neurobiology of intelligence. *Discovery Medicine, 4*(22), 157–162.

Hart, B., & Risley, T. R. (1995). *Meaningful differences in the everyday experience of young American children.* Baltimore: Paul H. Brookes Publishing.

Irvin, M. J., Meece, J. L., Byun, S., Farmer, T. W., & Hutchins, B. C. (2011). Relationship of school context to rural youth's educational achievement and aspirations. *Journal of Youth and Adolescence, 40*(9), 1225–1242.

Liston, C., McEwen, B. S., & Casey, B. J. (2009). Psychosocial stress reversibly disrupts prefrontal processing and attentional control. *Proceedings of the National Academy of Science, 106*(3), 912–917.

Menyuk, P. (1980). Effect of persistent otitis media on language development. *Annals of Otology, Rhinology, and Laryngology Supplement, 89*(3), 257–263.

Miller, E. M., Walton, G. M., Dweck, C. S., Job, V., Trzesniewski, K. H., & McClure, S. M. (2012). *Theories of willpower affect sustained learning. PLoS One, 7*(6), e38680.

Odéen, M., Westerlund, H., Theorell, T., Leineweber, C., Eriksen, H. R., & Ursin, H. (2012, February). Expectancies, socioeconomic status, and self-rated health. *International Journal of Behavioral Medicine.*

Paulussen-Hoogeboom, M. C., Stams, G. J., Hermanns, J. M., & Peetsma, T. T. (2007). Child negative emotionality and parenting from infancy to preschool. *Developmental Psychology, 43*(2), 438–453.

Risley, T. R., & Hart, B. (2006). Promoting early language development. In N. F. Watt, C. Ayoub, R. H. Bradley, J. E. Puma, & W. A. LeBoeuf (Eds.), *The crisis in youth mental health: Critical issues and effective programs, Volume 4, Early intervention programs and policies* (pp. 83–88). Westport, CT: Praeger.

Robb, K. A., Simon, A. E., & Wardle, J. (2009). Socioeconomic disparities in optimism and pessimism. *International Journal of Behavioral Medicine, 16*(4), 331–338.

Sargent, J., Brown, M. J., Freeman, J., Bailey, A., Goodman, D., & Freeman, D. (1995). Childhood lead poisoning in Massachusetts communities. *American Journal of Public Health, 85*(4), 528–534.

Spilt, J. L., Hughes, J. N, Wu, J., & Kwok, O. (2012). Child development, dynamics of teacher-student relationships. *Child Development, 83*(4), 1180–1195.

Taki, Y., Hashizume, H., Sassa, Y., Takeuchi, H., Asano, M., Asano, K., et al. (2010). Breakfast staple types affect brain gray matter volume and cognitive function in healthy children. *PLoS One, 5*(12), e15213.

Walker, D., Greenwood, C., Hart, B., & Carta, J. (1994). Prediction of school outcomes based on early language production and socioeconomic factors. *Child Development, 65*(2), 606–621.

Winter, B., Breitenstein, C., Mooren, F. C., Voelker, K., Fobker, M., Lechtermann, A., et al. (2007). High impact running improves learning. *Neurobiology of Learning and Memory, 87*(4), 597–609.

Yazzie-Mintz, E. (2007). National high school student engagement survey by IU reveals unengaged students [Press release]. Bloomington, Indiana State University. Retrieved from www.indiana.edu/~soenews/news/news1172622996.html

---

**Eric Jensen** (info@jlcbrain.com) is the author of *Engaging Students with Poverty in Mind* (ASCD, 2013) and *Teaching with Poverty in Mind* (ASCD, 2009); www.jensenlearning.com.

Originally published in the May 2013 issue of *Educational Leadership, 70*(8): pp. 24–30.

# Whose Problem Is Poverty?

Richard Rothstein

*It's no cop-out to acknowledge the effects of socioeconomic disparities on student learning. Rather, it's a vital step to closing the achievement gap.*

In my work, I've repeatedly stressed this logical claim: If you send two groups of students to equally high-quality schools, the group with greater socioeconomic disadvantage will necessarily have lower *average* achievement than the more fortunate group.[1]

Why is this so? Because low-income children often have no health insurance and therefore no routine preventive medical and dental care, leading to more school absences as a result of illness. Children in low-income families are more prone to asthma, resulting in more sleeplessness, irritability, and lack of exercise. They experience lower birth weight as well as more lead poisoning and iron-deficiency anemia, each of which leads to diminished cognitive ability and more behavior problems. Their families frequently fall behind in rent and move, so children switch schools more often, losing continuity of instruction.

Poor children are, in general, not read to aloud as often or exposed to complex language and large vocabularies. Their parents have low-wage jobs and are more frequently laid off, causing family stress and more arbitrary discipline. The neighborhoods through which these children walk to school and in which they play have more crime and drugs and fewer adult role models with professional careers. Such children are more often in single-parent families and so get less adult attention. They have fewer cross-country trips, visits to museums and zoos, music or dance lessons, and organized sports leagues to develop their ambition, cultural awareness, and self-confidence.

Each of these disadvantages makes only a small contribution to the achievement gap, but cumulatively, they explain a lot.

I've also noted that no matter how serious their problems, all disadvantaged students can expect to have higher achievement in better schools than in worse ones. And even in the same schools, natural human variability ensures a distribution of achievement in every group. Some high-achieving disadvantaged students always outperform typical middle class students, and some low-achieving middle class students fall behind typical disadvantaged students. The achievement gap is a difference in the *average* achievement of students from disadvantaged and middle class families.

I've drawn a policy conclusion from these observations: Closing or substantially narrowing achievement gaps requires combining school improvement with reforms that narrow the vast socioeconomic inequalities in the United States. Without such a combination, demands (like those of No Child Left Behind) that schools fully close achievement gaps not only will remain unfulfilled, but also will cause us to foolishly and unfairly condemn our schools and teachers.

## Distorting Disadvantage

Most educators understand how socioeconomic disadvantage lowers average achievement. However, some have resisted this logic, throwing up a variety of defenses. Some find in my explanations the implication that disadvantaged children have a genetic disability, that poor and minority children can't learn. They say that a perspective that highlights the socioeconomic causes of low achievement "blames the victim" and legitimizes racism. Some find my analysis dangerous because it "makes excuses" for poor instruction or because demands for social and economic reform "let schools off the hook" for raising student achievement. And others say it's too difficult to address nonschool problems like inadequate incomes, health, or housing, so we should only work on school reform. The way some of these critics see it, those of us who call attention to such nonschool issues must want to wait until utopian economic change (or "socialism") becomes a reality before we begin to improve schools.

Some critics cite schools that enroll disadvantaged students but still get high standardized test scores as proof that greater socioeconomic equality is not essential for closing achievement gaps—because good schools have shown they can do it on their own. And some critics are so single-mindedly committed to a schools-only approach that they can't believe anyone could seriously advocate pursuing *both* school and socioeconomic improvement simultaneously.

## Seeing Through "No Excuses"

The commonplace "no excuses" ideology implies that educators—were they to realize that their efforts alone were insufficient to raise student achievement—would be too simple-minded then to bring themselves to exert their full effort. The ideology presumes that policymakers with an Olympian perspective can trick teachers into performing at a higher level by making them believe that unrealistically high degrees of success are within reach.

There's a lack of moral, political, and intellectual integrity in this suppression of awareness of how social and economic disadvantage lowers achievement. Our first obligation should be to analyze social problems accurately; only then can we design effective solutions.

Presenting a deliberately flawed version of reality, fearing that the truth will lead to excuses, is not only corrupt but also self-defeating.

Mythology cannot, in the long run, inspire better instruction. Teachers see for themselves how poor health or family economic stress impedes students' learning. Teachers may nowadays be intimidated from acknowledging these realities aloud and may, in groupthink obedience, repeat the mantra that "all children can learn." But nobody is fooled. Teachers still know that although all children can learn, some learn less well because of poorer health or less-secure homes. Suppressing such truths leads only to teacher cynicism and disillusion. Talented teachers abandon the profession, willing to shoulder responsibility for their own instructional competence but not for failures beyond their control.

Mythology also prevents educators from properly diagnosing educational failure where it exists. If we expect all disadvantaged students to succeed at levels typical of affluent students, then even the best inner-city teachers seem like failures. If we pretend that achievement gaps are entirely within teachers' control, with claims to the contrary only "excuses," how can we distinguish better from worse classroom practice?

## Who's Getting Off the Hook?

Promoters of the myth that schools alone can overcome social and economic causes of low achievement assert that claims to the contrary let schools "off the hook." But their myth itself lets political and corporate officials off a hook. We absolve these leaders from responsibility for narrowing the pervasive inequalities of American society by asserting that good schools alone can overcome these inequalities. Forget about health care gaps, racial segregation, inadequate housing, or income insecurity. If, after successful school reform, all adolescents regardless of background could leave high school fully prepared to earn middle class incomes, there would, indeed, be little reason for concern about contemporary inequality. Opportunities of children from all races and

ethnic groups, and of rich and poor, would equalize in the next genera-
tion solely as a result of improved schooling. This absurd conclusion
follows from the "no excuses" approach.

Some critics urge that educators should not acknowledge socioeconomic disadvantage because their unique responsibility is to
improve classroom practices, which they *can* control. According to
such reasoning, we should leave to health, housing, and labor experts
the challenge of worrying about inequalities in their respective fields.
Yet we are all citizens in this democracy, and educators have a special
and unique insight into the damage that deprivation does to children's
learning potential.

If educators who face this unfortunate state of affairs daily don't
speak up about it, who will? Educators and their professional organizations should insist to every politician who will listen (and to those
who will not) that social and economic reforms are needed to create
an environment in which the most effective teaching can take place.

And yes, we should also call on housing, health, and antipoverty
advocates to take a broader view that integrates school improvement
into their advocacy of greater economic and social equality. Instead,
however, critical voices for reform have been silenced, told they should
stick to their knitting, fearing an accusation that denouncing inequality
is tantamount to "making excuses."

## What We Can Do

It's a canard that educators advocating socioeconomic reforms wish
to postpone school improvement until we have created an impractical economic utopia. Another canard is the idea that it's impractical
to narrow socioeconomic inequalities, so school reform is the only
reasonable lever. Modest social and economic reforms, well within our
political reach, could have a palpable effect on student achievement.
For example, we could

- Ensure good pediatric and dental care for all students, in school-based clinics.
- Expand existing low-income housing subsidy programs to reduce families' involuntary mobility.
- Provide higher-quality early childhood care so that low-income children are not parked before televisions while their parents are working.
- Increase the earned income tax credit, the minimum wage, and collective bargaining rights so that families of low-wage workers are less stressed.
- Promote mixed-income housing development in suburbs and in gentrifying cities to give more low-income students the benefits of integrated educations in neighborhood schools.
- Fund after-school programs so that inner-city children spend fewer nonschool hours in dangerous environments and, instead, develop their cultural, artistic, organizational, and athletic potential.

None of this is utopian. All is worth doing in itself, with the added benefit of sending children to school more ready to learn. Educators who are unafraid to advocate such policies will finally call the hand of those politicians and business leaders who claim that universal health care is too expensive but simultaneously demand school reform so they can posture as defenders of minority children.

In some schools, disadvantaged students are effectively tracked by race, denied the most qualified teachers and the best curriculum. Failure is both expected and accepted. Unfortunately, some educators do use socioeconomic disadvantage as an excuse for failing to teach well under adverse conditions. But we exaggerate the frequency of this excuse. Some teachers excuse poor practice, but others work terribly hard to develop disadvantaged students' talents. Where incompetence does exist, we should insist that school administrators root it out.

But consider this: The National Assessment of Educational Progress (NAEP), administered to a national student sample by the federal government, is generally considered the most reliable measure of U.S. students' achievement. Since 1990, the achievement gap between minority and white students has barely changed, feeding accusations that educators simply ignore the needs of minority youth. Yet average math scores of black 4th graders in 2007 were higher than those of white 4th graders in 1990 (National Center for Education Statistics, 2007, p. 10). If white achievement had been stagnant, the gap would have fully closed. There were also big math gains for black 8th graders (National Center for Education Statistics, 2007, p. 26). The gap stagnated only because white students also gained.

In reading, scores have remained flat. Perhaps this is because math achievement is a more direct result of school instruction, whereas reading ability also reflects students' home literacy environment. Nonetheless, the dramatic gains in math do not suggest that most teachers of disadvantaged students are sitting around making excuses for failing to teach. Quite the contrary.

## Reticent About Race

It is puzzling that some find racism implied in explanations of why disadvantaged students typically achieve at lower levels. But to understand that children who've been up at night, wheezing from untreated asthma, will be less attentive in school is not to blame those children for their lower scores. It is to explain that we can enhance those students' capacity to learn with policies that reduce the epidemic incidence of asthma in low-income communities—by enforcing prohibitions on the use of high-sulfur heating oil, for example, or requiring urban buses to substitute natural gas for diesel fuel—or provide pediatric care, including treatment for asthma symptoms. Denying the impact of poor health on learning leads to blaming teachers for circumstances completely beyond their control.

The fact that such conditions affect blacks more than whites reflects racism in the United States. Calling attention to such conditions is not racist. But ignoring them, insisting that they have no effect if teaching is competent, may be.

Some critics lump my analyses of social and economic obstacles with others' claims that "black culture" explains low achievement. Like other overly simplistic explanations of academic failure, cultural explanations can easily be exaggerated. There is, indeed, an apparent black-white test-score gap, even when allegedly poor black and white students are compared with one another or even when middle class black and white students are compared with one another. But these deceptively large gaps mostly stem from too-broad definitions of "poor" and "middle class." Typically, low-income white students are compared with blacks who are much poorer, and middle class black students are compared with whites who are much more affluent. If we restricted comparisons to socioeconomically similar students, the residual test-score gap would mostly disappear (see Phillips, Crouse, & Ralph, 1998).

But probably not all of it. Responsible reformers are seeking to help low-income black parents improve childrearing practices. Others attempt to reduce the influence of gang role models on black adolescents or to raise the status of academic success in black communities. Generally, these reformers are black; white experts avoid such discussions, fearing accusations of racism.

This is too bad. If we're afraid to discuss openly the small contribution that cultural factors make to achievement gaps, we suggest, falsely, that we're hiding something much bigger.

## Dancing Around the Issue

I am often asked to respond to claims that some schools with disadvantaged students have higher achievement, allegedly proving that schools alone *can* close achievement gaps. Certainly, some schools are superior and should be imitated. But no schools serving disadvantaged students have demonstrated consistent and sustained improvement that closes— not just narrows—achievement gaps. Claims to the contrary are often fraudulent, sometimes based on low-income schools whose parents are unusually well educated; whose admissions policies accept only the most talented disadvantaged students; or whose students, although eligible for subsidized lunches, come from stable working-class and not poor communities.

Some claims are based on schools that concentrate on passing standardized basic skills tests to the exclusion of teaching critical thinking, reasoning, the arts, social studies, or science, or of teaching the "whole child," as middle class schools are more wont to do. Increasingly, such claims are based on high proportions of students scoring above state proficiency standards, defined at a low level. Certainly, if we define proficiency down, we can more easily reduce achievement gaps without addressing social or economic inequality. But responsible analysts have always defined closing the achievement gap as achieving similar score distributions and average scale scores among subgroups. Even No Child Left Behind proclaims a goal of proficiency at "challenging" levels for each subgroup. Only achieving such goals will lead to more equal opportunity for all students in the United States.

## Beyond Either/Or

Nobody should be forced to choose between advocating for better schools or speaking out for greater social and economic equality. Both are essential. Each depends on the other. Educators cannot be effective if they make excuses for poor student performance. But they will have little chance for success unless they also join with advocates of social and economic reform to improve the conditions from which children come to school.

# Endnote

[1] For further discussion of this issue, see my book *Class and Schools: Using Social, Economic, and Educational Reform to Close the Black-White Achievement Gap* (Economic Policy Institute, 2004) and "The Achievement Gap: A Broader Picture" (*Educational Leadership*, November 2004).

# References

National Center for Education Statistics. (2007). *The nation's report card: Mathematics 2007*. Washington, DC: Author. Retrieved from http://nces.ed.gov/nationsreportcard/pdf/main2007/2007494.pdf

Phillips, M., Crouse, J., & Ralph, J. (1998). Does the black-white test score gap widen after children enter school? In C. Jencks & M. Phillips (Eds.), *The black-white test score gap* (pp. 229–272). Washington, DC: Brookings Institution Press.

**Richard Rothstein** (riroth@epi.org) is Research Associate at the Economic Policy Institute.

Originally published in the April 2008 issue of *Educational Leadership*, 65(7): pp. 8–13.

5

# On Savage Inequalities:
# A Conversation with Jonathan Kozol

Marge Scherer

*We ought to finance the education of every child in*
*America equitably, with adjustments made only for*
*the greater or lesser needs of certain children.*

Have you read *Savage Inequalities*? It's a question that comes up at
most educational conferences these days. The best-selling book by
Jonathan Kozol has touched many of the nation's educators and riled
others, including some notable politicians. In it, he compares rich and
poor schools located within a few miles of one another. The stark contrasts of physical surroundings and learning environments—in cities
and states from St. Louis to Detroit, New Jersey to Texas—bring home
a startling realization of just how different school can be for poor and
minority-race children as opposed to middle-class and white children.
In this interview with *Educational Leadership*, Kozol, a public school
advocate since his early teaching days, describes the conditions that
face our nation's urban students and suggests what we can do to eradi-
cate the inequities.

**In *Savage Inequalities*, you describe East St. Louis as the saddest place in the world. For the benefit of those who haven't read your book, would you please describe the conditions that you found there?**

Well, when I visited there a couple of years ago, East St. Louis was the poorest small city in America, virtually 100 percent black, a monument to apartheid in America. The city was so poor, there had been no garbage pickup for four years. There were heaps of garbage in the backyards of children's homes and thousands of abandoned automobile tires in empty lots.

On the edge of the city is a large chemical plant, Monsanto. There is also a very large toxic waste incinerator, as well as a huge sewage treatment plant. If you go there at night you see this orange-brownish smoke belching out of the smokestacks descending on the city. The soil is so toxic with mercury, lead, and zinc, as well as arsenic from the factories, that the city has one of the highest rates of infant mortality in Illinois, the highest rate of fetal death, and also a very high rate of childhood asthma.

The schools, not surprisingly, are utterly impoverished. East St. Louis High School, one of the two schools I visited, had a faint smell of water rot and sewage because not long before I visited, the entire school system had been shut down after being flooded with sewage from the city's antiquated sewage system. The physics teacher had no water in his physics lab—I remember that vividly. I was certainly stunned by that. In a city poisoned by several chemical plants, the science labs had very few chemicals. It was a scene of utter destitution.

I did meet several wonderful teachers in the school, and I thought the principal of the school was excellent. The superintendent of East St. Louis is also a very impressive person. In a sense, that sort of sums up the situation in many cities where I find great teachers and often very courageous administrators struggling against formidable odds, and then finding themselves condemned by venomous politicians in Washington for failing to promote excellence.

**You say that a primary reason that such conditions exist in public schools is inequitable funding. What kind of funding do you think would rectify the shocking conditions in the poorest schools? Are taxes too low? Are Americans not spending enough for public education?**

East St. Louis, like many poor cities in America, taxes itself at a very high rate. It's one of the most heavily taxed school districts in Illinois. In New Jersey, its counterpart is Camden. Camden has almost the highest property tax rate in New Jersey. But in both cases, because the property is virtually worthless, even with a high property tax, they cannot provide adequate revenues for their schools.

What we ought to do ultimately is get rid of the property tax completely as the primary means of funding public education, because it is inherently unjust. To use the local property tax as even a portion of school funding is unjust because it will always benefit the children of the most privileged people. The present system guarantees that those who can buy a $1 million home in an affluent suburb will also be able to provide their children with superior schools. That is a persistent betrayal of the whole idea of equal opportunity in America. It's a betrayal of democracy.

We ought to finance the education of every child in America equitably, with adjustments made only for the greater or lesser needs of certain children. And that funding should all come from the collective wealth of our society, mainly from a steeply graduated progressive income tax.

**Don't you think that financially able parents will always want to pay extra for the education of their children?**

Oh, sure. And if rich parents are afraid to let their children compete on an equal playing field, that's their right. But they ought to know what they're doing. They ought to recognize that they are protecting their children against democracy. And if they want to do that, they have a perfect right. They can pay $20,000 and send their kids to prep school. But they should not have that right within the public school system.

Even very conservative businessmen out in rich suburbs have in weak moments looked at me and said, "Well, you're right, we would never play Little League baseball this way." They wouldn't dream of sending their kids out with baseball mitts to play ball against a team that had to field the ball with bare hands. They'd regard that as being without honor. I say to them, "It's interesting. You wouldn't play baseball that way but you run the school system that way."

**A point that you make very clearly in your book is that the foundation program for schools provides a level of subsistence—a minimum, or basic education, but not an education on the level found in the rich or middle-class districts. What we have is not equal funding, but an equal minimum, and the rest of the funding is decided at the local level. You're saying that there's something very wrong with that?**

There are several things wrong with that. First of all, you guarantee every district—let's say, hypothetically, a basic minimum of $4,000. Then let's say a district that has enormous local wealth adds on another $4,000. That immediately invalidates the minimum $4,000 guarantee to the poor district because as soon as you double per-pupil spending, you raise the stakes. Now the rich district can steal away any teacher it wants. Many affluent people look at me and say, "Are you seriously telling us that if we want to spend more, we can't?" And I say: "That's right. Not in the public system. It isn't fair."

**Do you think that public schools are being abandoned today? For example, there are funding caps, arguments for vouchers for private schools, and efforts to create business-operated schools. Is support for public schools eroding?**

Absolutely. It's all part of the drive for privatizing the public sphere in the United States. It's a radical movement and it's very powerful. And it's not just in public education. It's part of a national pattern. In many big cities nowadays, affluent people vote against the taxes it would take to maintain good public parks and playgrounds. And then they spend the tax money they saved to join private health clubs, which they alone can enjoy. They vote against funds for citywide sanitation but then raise private funds to provide private sanitation simply for their exclusive neighborhood. They vote against taxation to increase citywide police protection and then hire expensive private security for their condominium. It's part of a pattern. The proposed voucher system is a larger extension of this pattern: cap the money for public schools and pull your own kids out.

**And you don't think the voucher system would help poor people in any way?**

No. Of course not. The voucher system is the most vicious possible device by which to enable affluent people and middle class people to flee the public system and to bring tax money with them into the private sector.

A $1,000 voucher, or even a $2,500 voucher, what will that buy a person? Can you buy tuition to Andover or Exeter or any other good prep school for that? Of course not. What can you do with that money? Well, if you're affluent, you could use that money to subsidize Andover tuition. If you're marginal middle class, that might just tip the balance and give you enough to pull off the tuition of a middle-grade private or parochial school. But if you're the poorest of the poor, you can't buy anything with $1,000. It's a sham to pretend to offer something to the poor when you're really offering a means for the middle class to rescue their children from the taint of the poor. The way I've heard it described is "save the best, and warehouse the rest."

What I find particularly bitter is that so many of the voucher advocates say, "Well, look. If these inner-city public schools were doing a good job, then we wouldn't be talking about vouchers." They say, "Look at these decrepit school buildings in East St. Louis. Look at these schools in Chicago that can't even afford toilet paper. That's why we need vouchers." But this is very cynical because the very same people who say this are the ones who voted for the politicians who starved our schools of adequate finances.

**I want to talk about practices that, in addition to equal funding, would improve the odds for low-income children in urban schools. What would make a difference for at-risk students?**

Well, let me just say parenthetically, while visiting urban schools, I saw some simply terrific teachers, some really wonderful school principals, and some excellent superintendents. But I purposely did not write a book where I highlighted these great exceptions because I've seen terrific exceptions for 25 years, and I don't want to waste my time pretending any longer that terrific exceptions represent a systemic answer to these problems. There are thousands of small victories every day in America, but I've seen too many small victories washed away by larger losses. School principals are always grateful if you write that kind of book, but I just didn't want to do it.

What would make a significant difference? Number 1: We ought to stop fooling around about preschool and do it at last after a quarter century. We ought to be providing full-day Head Start to every low-income child starting at the age of 2 ½. And make sure that every child gets that for at least two years, *every* low-income child. That's one thing.

Number 2: I would abolish the property tax as the basic means of funding and replace it, as I said before, by equitable funding for every American child deriving from a single federal source.

Number 3: I would provide an increment in funding for the low-income inner-city and rural schools. I would go even further and provide at least a $10,000 increment for any really superb, experienced teacher who agrees to teach in the inner city, not for one or two years when they're just out of college and it's sort of fun and exciting, but for a lifetime.

I would enact a one-time federal school reconstruction bill of about $100 billion to tear down all these decrepit school buildings and put up schools that children wouldn't be ashamed to enter in the morning. I would encourage the present drive for site-based management to increase local school autonomy. I would encourage the decentralization of school systems so that teachers, principals, parents, and sometimes students themselves could have more input into determination of curriculum, for example.

I would like to see a more sweeping decentralization of school administration, but in saying that, I want to be very cautious. I'm not implying that most of our school superintendents are incompetent, and I'm certainly not implying that inefficiency is the major problem in the public school system. There is a lot of inefficiency, but the big issue is abject destitution. It's a lack of enough money.

It's interesting. People will tell you big inner-city school systems are poorly administered and that there's a lot of waste. They never say that about the rich suburban school districts. The reason, of course, is that when you have $16,000 per pupil as they have in Great Neck, New York, for example, no one will ever know how inefficient you may be because there's plenty of money to waste. The spotlight shines only on the impoverished district.

**You mentioned site-based management. Many educators are urging that schools be restructured. They believe that site-based**

**management offers communities a chance to run schools more efficiently. Do you agree?**

I encourage more site-based management, but to me that's a secondary issue. The fact is that restructuring without addressing the extreme poverty of the inner-city schools—what will it get us? It will give us restructured destitution. And that's not a very significant gain. If the New York City schools were administered with maximum efficiency, without a single dollar wasted, they would still be separate and unequal schools. They would be more efficient segregated and unequal schools. But that's not a very worthy goal.

**Let's talk a little bit about curriculum innovations—for instance, the idea of reaching at-risk kids in ways that are usually reserved for the gifted. Teaching algebra to remedial students, for instance. Dissolving the tracking system. What are your opinions about these solutions to problems of inequity?**

Tracking! When I was a teacher, tracking had been thoroughly discredited. But during the past 12 years, tracking has come back with a vengeance. Virtually every school system I visit, with a few exceptions, is entirely tracked, although they don't use that word anymore. We have these cosmetic phrases like "homogeneous grouping." It's tracking, by whatever name, and I regret that very much. It's not just that tracking damages the children who are doing poorly, but it also damages the children who are doing very well, because, by separating the most successful students—who are often also affluent, white children—we deny them the opportunity to learn something about decency and unselfishness. We deny them the opportunity to learn the virtues of helping other kids. All the wonderful possibilities of peer teaching are swept away when we track our schools as severely as we are doing today.

The other thing, of course, is that tracking is so utterly predictive. The little girl who gets shoved into the low reading group in 2nd grade is very likely to be the child who is urged to take cosmetology instead of algebra in the 8th grade, and most likely to be in vocational courses, not college courses, in the 10th grade, if she hasn't dropped out by then. So, it's cruelly predictive. There's also a racist aspect to tracking. Black children are three times as likely as white children to be tracked into special-needs classes but only half as likely to be put in gifted programs. That's an intolerable statistic in a democracy. It's a shameful statistic. There's no possible way to explain it other than pure racism. It's one of the great, great scandals of American education.

**Some say that the real problem is not equity but excellence. What's your reaction to those who say we must not spend money until we know what really works in education?**

The problem is not that we don't know what works. The problem is that we are not willing to pay the bill to provide the things that work for the poorest children in America. And we have not been willing for many, many years. After all, if poor black parents on the South Side of Chicago want to know what works, they really don't need a $2 million grant from Exxon to set up another network of essential schools. All they need to do is to take a bus trip out to a high school in Wilmette and see what money pays for. All they need to do is go out and see schools where there are 16 children in a class with one very experienced teacher. All they need to do is visit a school with 200 IBMs; a school where the roof doesn't leak; a school that is surrounded by green lawns, where the architecture and atmosphere of the school entice people to feel welcome; a school in which the prosperity of the school creates the relaxed atmosphere in which the teachers feel free to innovate, which they seldom do under the conditions of filth and desperation.

What I'm saying is rather irreverent, I realize, but this is why I always sigh with weariness when I hear about the newest network of

effective, essential, or accelerated schools. I say, I've seen these proto-
type models come and go for years and they sure do make reputations
for the people who sponsor them. Foundations will support them and
business partners will get on board so long as it's in fashion. If the
issue in America were truly that we don't yet know what works, what
arrogance would lead us to believe that we are just now on the verge
of finding out?

**But critics of our schools are saying that there are schools that
have all kinds of equipment and materials and resources but
where the academic curriculum isn't very good, where kids aren't
learning that much. There are those who say the schools don't
need to be fixed for the poor children only; they need to be
systemically reformed to benefit all children. What about that
argument?**

I don't subscribe to the fashionable notion these days that all our
schools are failing. I don't buy the argument that it isn't just the poor
kids, it's all our kids; that suburban kids have it bad, too, and we need
to make these changes for everybody. I don't really think that's true.
It's a wonderfully consoling notion, because so long as it prevails, we
have a perfect justification for postponing any efforts toward equality. After all, if these kids in Great Neck are suffering as much as the
kids in the South Bronx, if all our schools are bad, if there's no way of
discriminating between lesser and greater forms of injustice, then we
can perpetuate the present inequalities for another century. I find that
a very disturbing notion.

Certainly, even at a top-rated, highly funded suburban high school,
there are a lot of things that I would like to change. There are kids at
such schools whose individuality is not adequately respected. There
are kids who suffer emotionally or don't get the challenging courses
of which they are capable. But let's put things in perspective. These

children are not by and large being destroyed for life. These children by and large are not going to end up in homeless shelters.

When people tell me that the schools in affluent suburbs are not doing the job that they could do, I ask, "Well, what do you mean by that?" Typically, they say, "Well, our daughter, Susan, went to our local school and she was bitterly short-changed academically. It did her real harm." And, I say, "What harm did it do her? Is she on welfare now?" "No," they say, "but she's having the devil of a time at Sarah Lawrence."

We've got to distinguish between injustice and inconvenience. Before we deal with an affluent child's existential angst, let's deal with the kid in Chicago who has not had a permanent teacher for the past five years.

It's a funny thing. After I give speeches, people will come up to me and say, "Good job." They seem to like me, but then a moment comes when they step away and I can tell something different is coming. That's the point where the question comes and the question is always the same. They ask, "Can you really solve this kind of problem with money? Is money really the answer?" I always think it's an amazing question. As though it's bizarre to suggest that money would be the solution to poverty. As though it's a bizarre idea that it would really take dollars to put a new roof on Morris High School in the Bronx and get the sewage out of the schools in East St. Louis; that it would take real money to hire and keep good teachers so they would stay for a lifetime in the schools that need them most; that it would take real money to buy computers. But that's what I always hear. They say, "Can you really solve this kind of problem by throwing money at it?" Conservatives love that word *throwing*. They never speak of throwing money at the Pentagon. We *allocate* money for the Pentagon. We throw money at anything that has to do with human pain. When they say that to me, I look them right in the eyes and say, "Sure. That's a great way to do it. Throw it. Dump it from a helicopter. Put it in my pocket and I'll bring it to the school myself." I don't know a better way to fix the root problem.

**What is it that got you involved in public schools—and fighting injustice?**

Oh, who knows? My mother read the Bible to me when I was a child. She's a very religious Jewish woman. My father is a physician; he spent much of his life healing poor people. My entire education was in English literature at Harvard and Oxford, and I got into teaching quite by accident. It was the spring of 1964. Three young men were murdered in Mississippi: Schwerner, Chaney, and Goodman. I was shaken by that, particularly by the death of Michael Schwerner, since he was from a background very much like mine, middle-class Jewish family from the North. So I got on the train at Harvard Square and went to the end of the line, to Roxbury, the ghetto of Boston, and signed up to teach a Freedom School, run by the Civil Rights Movement.

That was in the summer, and in the fall, I signed up as a teacher in the Boston public schools. Although I wasn't certified, I was told that if I did not mind teaching black children, I could go into the classroom. That was a quick introduction to American racism. The year ended with my being fired.

**Because you tried to teach Robert Frost and Langston Hughes and they weren't in the curriculum?**

Yes. I was hired a couple of years later to teach in one of the wealthiest suburban school districts outside of Boston. There I saw what good education can be, what wonderful conditions can exist for privileged children. That's when, in a sense, this book that I just published, began. I saw how unfairly our schools are financed and governed. That hasn't changed. It's very much the same today. It's worse in many ways because there are so few political leaders even questioning these inequalities. I might just say parenthetically, the reason I made some critical references before to some of those pedagogic figures who get a lot of money to set up networks of excellent, accelerated, essential, or effective schools, the reason I refer to that with a sense of reservation, is that these people would not get that kind of foundation money if they were speaking candidly about racism and inequality. In order to make their programs palatable, they have substituted an agenda of innovation for an agenda of justice.

Listen, I've been invited to probably 100 conferences on education since this book was published. I've been to conferences on "quality" in education, on "more effective" education, on "excellence in education." I have not been invited to one conference on *equality in education*. There are no such conferences. And yet that remains the central issue in American education, as it does in American democracy. That troubles me very much. To be honest, I'm surprised this book became a bestseller. I don't know why it did.

**Where did you get the title, *Savage Inequalities*?**

I chose that title because I was sick of powerful people suggesting that there was some kind of essential savagery in poor black children in America. I wanted to make clear that if there is something savage in America, it is in the powerful people who are willing to tolerate these injustices. That's why I chose it. I agree it's a tough title, and some people tried to talk me out of it, but I stuck with it.

---

**Jonathan Kozol** is author of *Savage Inequalities: Children In America's Schools* (Crown Publishers, Inc. 1991). **Marge Scherer** is Editor in Chief of *Educational Leadership*.

Originally published in the December 1992/January 1993 issue of *Educational Leadership*, *50*(4): pp. 4–9.

6

# Boosting Achievement by Pursuing Diversity

Halley Potter

*What can we learn from schools that are improving student achievement by breaking up concentrated student poverty?*

One morning last December, a crowd gathered at the Thomas B. Fordham Institute in Washington, D.C., for a discussion on school turnaround. Panelists debated whether the best way to fix persistently underperforming schools was simply to replace the administrators and teachers at the school, or whether reopening under new charter management was the only effective option.

But what if, instead of changing the principal, teachers, or management in the hope that this will turn around a high-poverty school, we changed the mix of students, rebalancing enrollment so that the school did not serve a concentration of the most disadvantaged students? When asked this question, panelist Carmel Martin, assistant secretary for the U.S. Department of Education, said, "I think it's a really important question." But she quickly added, "We're focused on governance and the people [adults] in the building, which we think are critical ingredients."

Although few policymakers and wonks are talking about it, a small but growing number of schools are attempting to boost the achievement of low-income students by shifting enrollment to place more low-income students in mixed-income schools. Socioeconomic integration is an effective way to tap into the academic benefits of having high-achieving peers, an engaged community of parents, and high-quality teachers.

In the last decade, the number of public school districts that consider socioeconomic status in student assignment has grown from just a handful to more than 80 (Kahlenberg, 2012). Early adopters included La Crosse, Wisconsin, which created a districtwide plan to balance school enrollment by socioeconomic status in 1979, and Cambridge, Massachusetts, which made socioeconomic status the main factor in its controlled choice program in 2001. Newer additions include Bloomington, Minnesota, and Salina, Kansas, both of which used socioeconomic balance as a factor in redrawing school boundaries in recent years.

Adding to this list, a number of charter schools now actively seek socioeconomically diverse student enrollment as part of their design. They include schools like High Tech High, which began in 2000 as a single charter school and is now a network of 11 schools in San Diego, and Citizens of the World Charter Schools, which opened its first school in 2010 and is striving to create a national network of diverse charter schools.

Going against the grain in a country where many public schools are de facto segregated by income, these socioeconomically integrated charter schools have developed innovative methods for enrolling and serving a diverse student body.

## The Case for Socioeconomic Integration

On average, students' socioeconomic backgrounds have a huge effect on their academic outcomes. But so do the backgrounds of the peers who surround them. Poor students in mixed-income schools do better than poor students in high-poverty schools.

Research supporting socioeconomic integration goes back to the famous Coleman Report, which found that the strongest school-related predictor of student achievement was the socioeconomic composition of the student body (Coleman et al., 1966). More recent data confirm the relationship between individual achievement and student-body characteristics. A 2010 meta-analysis found that students of all socioeconomic statuses, races, ethnicities, and grade levels were likely to have higher mathematics performance if they attended socioeconomically and racially integrated schools (Mickelson & Bottia, 2010). And results of the 2011 National Assessment of Educational Progress in mathematics show steady increases in low-income 4th graders' average scores as the percentage of poor students in their school decreases (U.S. Department of Education, 2011).

Of course, multiple non-school-related factors could explain why low-income students in mixed-income schools outperform their counterparts in high-poverty schools. Students attending mixed-income schools might be more likely to have involved parents or live in a more affluent community, for example. However, a number of studies have found that the relationship between student outcomes and the socioeconomic composition of schools is strong even after controlling for some of these factors, using more nuanced measures of socioeconomic status, or comparing outcomes for students randomly assigned to schools (Reid, 2012; Schwartz, 2012).

Socioeconomic integration improves student outcomes because mixed-income schools are more likely to have certain resources or characteristics that foster achievement. Rumberger and Palardy (2005) found that the socioeconomic composition of the school was as strong a predictor of student outcomes as students' own socioeconomic status. However, the researchers found that the advantages of attending a mixed-income school could be fully explained by school characteristics such as teachers' expectations, students' homework habits, and school safety. They concluded that high-poverty schools could work "*if* it were possible to alter those policies and practices that are associated with schools' socioeconomic composition" (p. 2021).

That *if* is a serious caveat. High-performing, high-poverty schools are very rare. The economist Douglas Harris (2007) calculated that only 1.1 percent of majority-low-income schools consistently performed in the top third of their state. Further, to the extent that the biggest advantage of socioeconomic integration may be direct peer effects (Reid, 2012)—picking up knowledge and habits from high-achieving, highly motivated peers—high-poverty schools will always be at a disadvantage, given the strong relationship between students' own socioeconomic statuses and their academic performance.

Socioeconomic integration is a win-win situation: Low-income students' performance rises; all students receive the cognitive benefits of a diverse learning environment (Antonio et al., 2004; Phillips, Rodosky, Muñoz, & Larsen, 2009); and middle-class students' performance seems to be unaffected up to a certain level of integration. Research about this last point is still developing. A recent meta-analysis found "growing but still inconclusive evidence" that the achievement of more advantaged students was not harmed by desegregation policies (Harris, 2008, p. 563). It appears that there is a tipping point, a threshold for the proportion of low-income students in a school below which middle-class achievement does not suffer.

Estimates of this tipping point vary; many researchers cite 50 percent low-income as the maximum (Kahlenberg, 2001). However, in a report that Richard Kahlenberg and I coauthored for the Century Foundation, we profiled diverse charter schools in which the proportion of low-income students (as measured by eligibility for free and reduced-price lunch) ranged from 30 to 70 percent, within 20 percentage points of the 50 percent goal (Kahlenberg & Potter, 2012). The findings suggested that, more than a precise threshold, what mattered in these schools was maintaining a critical mass of middle-class families, which promoted a culture of high expectations, safety, and community support.

## Lessons from Socioeconomically Diverse Charter Schools

Despite the evidence of their advantages, socioeconomically integrated schools are not the norm in the United States. In traditional public schools, 65 percent of low-income students are concentrated in majority-low-income schools. In charter schools, that figure is 78 percent (Frankenberg, Siegel-Hawley, & Wang, 2010).

Many choices have led to our economically segregated school system.[1] Districts have chosen to let school boundaries reflect or even amplify residential segregation. Reformers have chosen to focus more on fixing high-poverty schools than on breaking up concentrations of poverty. Policymakers and philanthropists have favored interventions targeted at reaching as many low-income students as possible. But de facto school segregation also persists because balancing student enrollment by socioeconomic status, like most education reforms, is logistically, politically, and operationally difficult.

Socioeconomically diverse charter schools are developing practices to overcome some of the challenges of enrolling and serving a diverse student body. They have identified strategies that could help other schools and districts create successful integration programs.

### Enrolling a Diverse Student Body

One of the foremost logistical barriers to integrating schools by socioeconomic status is geography. Residential poverty tends to be concentrated, and successful school integration requires either a district with enough socioeconomic diversity within its boundaries or a group of neighboring districts which, when combined, have enough diversity to facilitate an interdistrict integration plan. The availability of these geographic opportunities varies widely in states across the country (Mantil, Perkins, & Aberger, 2012).

Some diverse charter schools were started by first identifying a geographic opportunity for integration that traditional public schools were neglecting. For example, Blackstone Valley Prep Mayoral Academy serves four adjacent Rhode Island communities, drawing students evenly from two higher-income suburbs and two lower-income cities. Larchmont Charter School in Los Angeles, California, was started by a group of parents from Hollywood who were frustrated that the demographics of their community, one of the most diverse neighborhoods in L.A., were not reflected in the area's schools.

Political opposition to adjusting attendance boundaries is another challenge. In Wake County, North Carolina, frequent student reassignments created controversy over the school district's long-standing socioeconomic integration plan. Opposition culminated in 2010, when a Tea Party–backed majority on the school board voted to end the plan. This group, however, was replaced in the next election by a prointegration majority. Similar backlash greeted a new school-boundary plan in Eden Prairie, Minnesota, that also balanced students by socioeconomic status.

Some charter schools pursuing socioeconomic integration have shown how systems of school choice can be used to foster diversity as an alternative to redrawing attendance zones. A weighted lottery is the simplest way for schools to ensure that they enroll a diverse student body while still relying on choice-based enrollment. For example, DSST Public Schools, a network of charter middle and high schools in Denver, Colorado, reserves a minimum of 40 percent of seats at the flagship campus for low-income students; Blackstone Valley Prep in Rhode Island reserves 60 percent of seats. High Tech High weights admissions lotteries in its elementary, middle, and high schools by students' home zip codes, which creates socioeconomically, racially, and ethnically diverse student bodies because of housing patterns.

Choice-based schools can also maintain a diverse balance by intentionally targeting underrepresented groups of students when publicizing their school. Capital City Public Charter School and E. L. Haynes Public Charter School are both located in Washington, D.C., where weighted lotteries are not permitted. Both schools maintain socioeconomically diverse enrollment through strategic recruitment for the lottery pool. E. L. Haynes, for example, receives many applications from middle-class families who proactively seek information because of the school's reputation, and it therefore directs all its recruitment efforts—from distributing information outside grocery stores to speaking at neighborhood association meetings—to low-income communities.

## Serving a Diverse Student Body

Once an integration strategy is in place, schools and teachers must also adapt to serve a diverse group of students. Mixed-income schools can draw criticism from both directions with respect to how well the school community and individual classrooms are integrated. On the one hand, students in diverse schools are sometimes separated into tracked classes along lines that mirror socioeconomic status, and students may further self-segregate during free time. In that situation, middle-income and low-income students are cheated out of some of the peer interactions and access to broader social networks that diversity can offer. On the other hand, schools that intentionally maintain heterogeneous classes must consider the research suggesting that these classes can negatively affect the academic progress of higher achievers (Brewer, Rees, & Argys, 1995).

Individual success stories and a review of research suggest that it is possible, by offering all students a single challenging curriculum, to reduce the achievement gap without harming the highest achievers (Burris, Wiley, Welner, & Murphy, 2008; Rui, 2009). However, ability grouping remains a hotly debated topic that is particularly relevant at socioeconomically diverse schools, where students enter school with a wide range of knowledge and skills (see Petrilli, 2012). How can mixed-income schools best support lower-achieving students without hurting the higher achievers?

High Tech High and City Neighbors Charter School have innovative strategies for blending the benefits of leveled instruction and heterogeneous classrooms. High Tech High is committed to grouping students by mixed ability as much as possible. "It's not just diversity in admissions," said CEO Larry Rosenstock. "It's also integration in practice once they've arrived." Leaders at High Tech High realized they needed to offer honors classes so that students could have the weighted grade point averages that selective colleges look for in admissions, but they did not want to separate the highest-achieving students from their peers. Instead, they offer some classes with an honors option, allowing interested students to take the class at the honors level by completing extra assignments.

At City Neighbors Charter School, a K–8 school in Baltimore, Maryland, teachers regularly adjust student groupings to ensure that all students are appropriately supported and challenged. In the lower grades, students may sometimes be grouped into similar-ability reading circles; but for most assignments, they work in heterogeneous groups chosen for their members' complementary skill sets. Monica O'Gara, a 1st grade teacher and founding faculty member, described the range of student backgrounds as both a challenge and a resource: "There's quite a mix of what children understand and what approaches they're used to or will be effective with them." Although differentiation is a challenge for teachers, students of all backgrounds benefit from hearing about their classmates' experiences and from relating their own experiences to others.

In the middle grades, students at City Neighbors start their day with half an hour of highly specialized, small-group instruction called *intensive*. Intensive provides an opportunity for extra support or enrichment in different subjects, allowing teachers to meet different students' needs while still teaching most of the academic time in mixed-ability classrooms. For example, some students may spend their intensive time receiving extra writing support while others attend an enrichment intensive on animal dissection. Students cycle through different intensives three times a year, giving teachers multiple opportunities to adjust placements based on individual needs.

Some charter schools are also tackling the more elusive issue of how to encourage students of different backgrounds to interact socially. Community Roots Charter School, an elementary and middle school in Brooklyn, created a staff position—director of community development—to facilitate programs that promote community cohesion and celebrate diversity. Through the school's Play and Learning Squads, for example, small groups of students and their parents go on weekend or afternoon outings. Teachers assign the squads with an eye toward grouping students who would not otherwise spend time together outside school.

## A Promising Direction

Academic results from these diverse charter schools are promising, if anecdotal. In our Century Foundation report, Richard Kahlenberg and I (2012) profiled seven diverse charter schools whose low-income students outperformed their low-income peers statewide in mathematics and reading, sometimes by dramatic margins. In all but one case, the schools' low-income students also beat the state proficiency averages for all students.

Many factors are at work in successful diverse charter schools. As schools of choice, these schools likely benefit from having a more engaged parent community than neighboring traditional public schools do. Still, when combined with the body of research showing the academic advantages of providing mixed-income learning environments, their stories are hopeful. If more schools, charter and otherwise, use creative strategies to tackle the challenges of socioeconomic integration, they can help shift the turnaround discussion from an exclusive focus on how to improve high-poverty schools to a discussion that also looks seriously at how to break up concentrations of poverty and provide more diverse learning environments for all students.

## Endnote

[1] See Richard Rothstein's article in the May 2013 issue of *Educational Leadership* for a discussion of the societal causes of segregation in U.S. schools.

## References

Antonio, A. L., Chang, M. J., Hakuta, K., Kenny, D. A., Levin, S., & Milem, J. F. (2004). Effects of racial diversity on complex thinking in college students. *Psychological Science, 15*(8), 507–510.

Brewer, D. J., Rees, D. I., & Argys, L. M. (1995). Detracking America's schools: The reform without cost? *Phi Delta Kappan, 77*(3), 210–212, 214–215.

Burris, C. C., Wiley, E. W., Welner, K. G., & Murphy, J. (2008). Accountability, rigor, and detracking: Achievement effects of embracing a challenging curriculum as a universal good for all students. *Teachers College Record, 110*(3), 571–608.

Coleman, J. S., Campbell, E. Q., Hobson, C. J., McPartland, J., Mood, J. M., Weinfeld, F. D., et al. (1966). *Equality of educational opportunity.* Washington, DC: U.S. Department of Health, Education, and Welfare, Office of Education/ National Center for Education Statistics.

Frankenberg, E., Siegel-Hawley, G., & Wang, J. (2010). *Choice without equity: Charter school segregation and the need for civil rights standards.* Los Angeles: Civil Rights Project at UCLA.

Harris, D. (2007). High-flying schools, student disadvantage, and the logic of NCLB. *American Journal of Education, 113*(3), 367–394.

Harris, D. (2008). Educational outcomes of disadvantaged students: From desegregation to accountability. In H. F. Ladd & E. B. Fiske (Eds.), *Handbook of research in education finance and policy* (pp. 551–572). New York: Routledge.

Kahlenberg, R. D. (2001). *All together now: Creating middle-class schools through public school choice.* Washington, DC: Brookings Institution Press.

Kahlenberg, R. D. (2012). Introduction: Socioeconomic school integration. In R. D. Kahlenberg (Ed.), *The future of school integration: Socioeconomic diversity as an education reform strategy* (pp. 1–26). New York: Century Foundation Press.

Kahlenberg, R. D., & Potter, H. (2012). *Diverse charter schools: Can racial and socioeconomic integration promote better outcomes for students?* Washington, DC, and New York: Poverty and Race Research Action Council and Century Foundation. Retrieved from http://tcf.org/assets/downloads/Diverse_Charter_Schools.pdf

Mantil, A., Perkins, A. G., & Aberger, S. (2012). The challenge of high-poverty schools: How feasible is socioeconomic school integration? In R. D. Kahlenberg (Ed.), *The future of school integration: Socioeconomic diversity as an education reform strategy* (pp. 155–222). New York: Century Foundation Press.

Mickelson, R. S., & Bottia, M. (2010). Integrated education and mathematics outcomes: A synthesis of social science research. *North Carolina Law Review*, *87*, 993–1089.

Petrilli, M. J. (2012). *The diverse schools dilemma: A parent's guide to socioeconomically mixed public schools*. Washington, DC: Fordham Institute.

Phillips, K. J. R., Rodosky, R. J., Muñoz, M. A., & Larsen, E. S. (2009). Integrated schools, integrated futures? A case study of school desegregation in Jefferson County, Kentucky. In C. E. Smrekar & E. B. Goldring (Eds.), *From the courtroom to the classroom: The shifting landscape of school desegregation* (pp. 239–270). Cambridge, MA: Harvard Education Press.

Reid, J. L. (2012). Socioeconomic diversity and early learning: The missing link in policy for high-quality preschools. In R. D. Kahlenberg (Ed.), *The future of school integration: Socioeconomic diversity as an education reform strategy* (pp. 67–126). New York: Century Foundation Press.

Rui, N. (2009). Four decades of research on the effects of detracking reform: Where do we stand? *Journal of Evidence-Based Medicine, 2*(3), 164–183.

Rumberger, R. W., & Palardy, G. J. (2005). Does segregation still matter? The impact of student composition on academic achievement in high school. *Teachers College Record, 107*(9), 1999–2045.

Schwartz, H. (2012). Housing policy is school policy: Economically integrative housing promotes academic success in Montgomery County, Maryland. In R. D. Kahlenberg (Ed.), *The future of school integration: Socioeconomic diversity as an education reform strategy* (pp. 27–66). New York: Century Foundation Press.

U.S. Department of Education, Institute of Education Sciences, National Center for Education Statistics. (2011). *National Assessments of Educational Progress (NAEP), 2011 math assessment, grade 4*. Data generated using the NAEP Data Explorer at http://nces.ed.gov/nationsreportcard/naepdata

**Halley Potter** (potter@tcf.org) is policy associate for the Century Foundation in Washington, D.C.

Originally published in the May 2013 issue of *Educational Leadership, 70*(8): pp. 38–43.

# When Mobility Disrupts Learning

Jean Louise M. Smith, Hank Fien, and Stan C. Paine

*Using proactive strategies, schools can reduce the
adverse academic effects of student mobility.*

As schools struggle to improve the reading achievement of *all* students, one factor that often impedes their success is student mobility. Unfortunately, mobility is a common phenomenon that disproportionately affects students in high-poverty schools.

A U.S. General Accounting Office (1994) study found that 40 percent of 3rd grade students in the United States had moved at least once between 1st and 3rd grade; 17 percent of those students had changed schools at least twice during that time. More recently, Rumberger (2003) analyzed 1998 data and found that 34 percent of 4th graders, 21 percent of 8th graders, and 10 percent of 12th graders had changed schools at least once in the previous two years. Fourth grade students in poor families were much more likely to have changed schools in the last two years (43 percent) than were students in nonpoor families (26 percent).

## The Effects of Student Mobility

Student mobility has "potentially deep and pervasive consequences" for individual students and the schools they attend (Kerbow, 1996, p. 1). Mobility can harm students' nutrition and health, increase grade retention, and lower academic achievement (U.S. General Accounting Office, 1994; Wood, Halfon, Scarlata, Newacheck, & Nessim, 1993). High student-mobility rates can also disrupt the learning environment in the classroom and throughout the school (Lash & Kirkpatrick, 1990).

Research is especially clear about the effects of mobility on academic skills, such as reading. When students move repeatedly, their reading skills often fall further and further behind those of their peers (Alexander, Entwisle, & Dauber, 1996; Kerbow, 1996; Nelson, Simoni, & Adelman, 1996). Without intervention, highly mobile students are likely to experience reading difficulty throughout their school careers and, indeed, throughout their lives (Juel, 1988; Vellutino, Scanlon, & Spearing, 1995).

To illustrate the effects of student mobility on reading achievement, Figure 7.1 shows the spring reading performance of 2,289 2nd

| Figure 7.1: Reading Performance of Stable and Mobile 2nd Grade Students | | | | | | |
|---|---|---|---|---|---|---|
| | Level of Stability | | | | | |
| | More ← | | | | | → Less |
| | Group A (n = 1077) | | Group B (n = 945) | | Group C (n = 267) | |
| Spring Measure | M | SD | M | SD | M | SD |
| DIBELS Oral Reading Fluency | 93.5 | 33.1 | 84.0 | 39.8 | 75.4 | 40.6 |
| Stanford Achievement Test | 594.2 | 39.3 | 585.0 | 42.8 | 577.3 | 40.8 |

Note: Group A: Students who attended the same school from kindergarten through 2nd grade. Group B: Students who attended the same school during 2nd grade. Group C: Students who moved into a school in the middle of 2nd grade. M - Mean SD - Standard deviation grade students who attended 34 schools across Oregon during the 2005–06 school year. The selected schools served high-poverty populations, had a history of poor student-reading outcomes, and were engaged in a multiyear school reform effort. Students in Group A attended the same school across three years, from kindergarten through 2nd grade; those in Group B attended 2nd grade in the same school across one year; and those in Group C moved into a school in the middle of 2nd grade. As measured by the Dynamic Indicators of Basic Early Literacy Skills (DIBELS) Oral Reading Fluency Assessment and the Stanford Achievement Test, reading performance increased the longer a student stayed in a particular school. The differences in scores among the three groups were statistically significant.

## Strategies for Success

For many schools—especially those serving high-poverty communities—the discontinuity caused by student mobility is a constant phenomenon. The most successful schools acknowledge the problem and implement schoolwide reading systems to provide instructional support for all students, including students who move into the school midyear (Simmons et al., 2002). An example is the Bethel School District in Eugene, Oregon, whose seven elementary schools have student-mobility rates ranging from 8 percent to 21 percent. The proportion of students eligible for free and reduced-price lunch in these schools ranges from 30 percent to 76 percent.

The Bethel School District began implementing schoolwide and districtwide reading systems more than a decade ago, after analyzing reading data and noticing a discrepancy between the reading achievement of mobile students and that of their peers. Knowing that the causes of student mobility were largely beyond their control, district staff members implemented strategies to reduce the harmful effects of mobility on students' reading achievement. The following strategies have been particularly effective in the Bethel School District and others like it.

## Implement an Enrollment Plan

Student records often do not transfer to the new school until days or weeks after the student arrives. In the meantime, teachers have difficulty matching the student with appropriate instruction. Schools can use two strategies to smooth the transition for students and their teachers.

First, assign a staff member to call the previous school as soon as a new student enrolls to gather information about the student's academic experiences. To put this strategy in place, a school team can develop a brief interview form that includes the following questions to ask the previous school:

- What are the student's academic strengths?
- Was the student in any special program at your school (for example, speech/language services, before/after school programs, gifted services, English language development, or academic support services)?
- What was the student's reading and math instruction like at your school (specific programs, amount of time, instructional approach, and so on)?
- Did the student have any attendance problems while at your school?
- Do you have any academic concerns regarding the student?

Second, use screening measures to quickly get an indication of the student's current reading skills and instructional needs. If the student's initial screening and interview information suggests that he or she is significantly behind grade-level expectations, a school team may convene to discuss the types of support the student will need to be successful.

The key to the effectiveness of both of these strategies is preplanning. The involved staff members should know their roles and be familiar with the process so that the transition happens smoothly and quickly. When developing an enrollment plan, a school should consider who will make the phone call to the previous school (for example, the student's new classroom teacher, the principal, or the school counselor) and who will be responsible for assessing the student's reading skills (for example, the school psychologist, speech pathologist, reading specialist, teacher, or someone else who has received appropriate training in the screening measures).

## Implement a Schoolwide Instructional Support Plan

Schools with highly mobile student populations should have a schoolwide, multitiered instructional support plan in place. That way, the school can place students who come into the school midyear in the instructional group, reading program, and tier of support that initial screening has determined will best fit their needs. The plan should allow school teams to systematically differentiate instruction for students who are successfully meeting reading goals, students who are at *some* risk for not meeting goals, and students who are at *high* risk for not meeting goals.

To address the instructional needs of mobile students who are at risk, schools can increase the amount of instructional time, decrease group size, and use instructional programs that are specifically designed to catch students up to grade-level expectations. It is essential that instruction for these students incorporate proven strategies. A recent synthesis commissioned by the Institute of Education Sciences found moderate to strong evidence for the effectiveness of the following methods: spacing learning over time, combining graphic and verbal descriptions, connecting abstract and concrete representations of concepts, using formative assessment, and using prequestions to introduce a topic (Pashler et al., 2007).

Even with strong schoolwide instructional support plans in place, schools sometimes run into the problem of students enrolling midyear who are too far behind to fit into existing reading groups. A Bethel administrator explains the strategy for such students:

Rather than refer them for special education services, these students have been placed in an intensive reading program based on scientifically based reading research; they receive two to three lessons per day, and they have made phenomenal gains.

It is essential that instructional groupings be flexible to respond to students' different learning rates. At monthly (or more frequent) grade-level team meetings, teachers should regroup students on the basis of their progress. Grouping should also recognize the specific skills students need to develop proficiency—for example, phonemic awareness, decoding, or comprehension.

## Implement a Coordinated Assessment Plan

Flexible grouping depends on having a coordinated assessment plan in place that not only screens students initially but also regularly identifies current skills, monitors progress, and periodically reviews important outcomes. The assessment plan and schoolwide instructional support plan must be integrated.

When creating a coordinated assessment plan, the school team should consider several questions for each grade level:

- What reliable and valid assessment tools are already in place?
- Do the types of assessment now in place meet the multiple purposes of assessment (screening, progress monitoring, identifying current skills, and tracking important outcomes)?
- Where do we need to implement new assessment tools?
- Who needs training on the different assessment tools?
- When will initial and ongoing professional development occur?
- What is the most effective and efficient way to manage assessment data and create useful reports?
- How will the data be disseminated and used?

To support the schoolwide assessment plan, teachers should prepare extra assessment materials ahead of time to smooth the transition as students move into instructional groups. They should use assessment results to make data-based decisions about student grouping. It is helpful if each teacher maintains a notebook containing assessment materials and individual student performance data that is readily available for grade-level team meetings.

## Additional Supports

In addition to schoolwide instructional plans, school districts can ease transitions for highly mobile students by developing consistent curriculum and instruction and by building ties with families.

In some communities, students frequently move between schools within the same district. Having similar instructional programs, assessment systems, and expectations at all schools provides a consistent program for students, makes program placement easier for teachers, and enables schools to align screening and progress-monitoring activities as well as professional development.

Establishing ongoing, effective communication with families of students who frequently move between schools can be challenging. Such homeschool linkages, however, can give the school valuable information about the student and involve parents as active agents in the transition process. Schools can use the following strategies to reach out to all families, including those who are new to the school or district:

- Organize a family resource center in the school. Include educational materials in multiple languages.
- Identify parent liaisons (including some who speak families' home languages) who can effectively explain the school's reading program to parents.
- Identify a staff member who can check in with each new student (and family) frequently during the student's first weeks

in the school. This person can help establish a bond among the student, family, and school and may also be able to recommend attendance and behavior programs when appropriate.

- Establish an attendance incentive program. Families who move a great deal may not enroll their children in their new school right away and may not see school attendance as a high priority.
- Schedule a parent conference within a few weeks of the student's enrollment. If needed, have a translator available who can describe the student's progress and instructional plan.

## Focus on Problem Solving

It is easy for educators to blame a student's frequent moves on the instability of the family and to conclude that the cycle of moving and falling behind academically are inevitable. When educators give in to this temptation, team meetings can quickly deteriorate from problem-solving sessions to long discussions of the complicated circumstances surrounding an individual student's lack of academic success. Instead of "admiring the problem" in this way (Ysseldyke & Christenson, 1988), school teams should focus on identifying and modifying the factors that are within their control.

A commitment to screening students immediately on enrollment, thoughtfully placing them into flexible instructional groups, monitoring their progress, and adjusting instruction as needed can accelerate learning and thereby provide students with a new opportunity to succeed in school. Developing consistent districtwide curriculums and building strong ties between school and home can provide additional support for mobile students. Believing that we can make a difference in all students' academic development, regardless of how long they might be with us, brings out the best in educators.

# References

Alexander, K., Entwisle, D., & Dauber, S. (1996). Children in motion: School transfers and elementary school performance. *Journal of Educational Research, 90*(1), 3–12.

Juel, C. (1988). Learning to read and write: A longitudinal study of 54 children from first through fourth grades. *Journal of Educational Psychology, 80*, 437–447.

Kerbow, D. (1996). *Patterns of urban student mobility and local school reform* (Tech. Rep. No. 5), Chicago: University of Chicago.

Lash, A. A., & Kirkpatrick, S. L. (1990). A classroom perspective on student mobility. *Elementary School Journal, 91*(2), 173.

Nelson, P., Simoni, J., & Adelman, H. (1996). Mobility and school functioning in the early grades. *Journal of Educational Research, 89*(6), 365–369.

Pashler, H., Bain P., Bottge, B., Graesser, A., Koedinger, K., McDaniel, M., & Metcalfe, J. (2007). *Organizing instruction and study to improve student learning* (NCER 2007-2004). Washington, DC: Institute for Education Sciences, U.S. Department of Education. Available at http://ies.ed.gov/ncee/wwc/pdf/20072004.pdf

Rumberger, R. W. (2003). The causes and consequences of student mobility. *Journal of Negro Education, 72*(1), 6–21.

Simmons, D. C., Kame'enui, E. J., Good, R. H., Harn, B. A., Cole, C., & Braun, D. (2002). Building, implementing, and sustaining a beginning reading improvement model school by school and lessons learned. In M. Shinn, G. Stoner, & H. M. Walker (Eds.), *Interventions for academic and behavior problems II: Preventive and remedial approaches* (pp. 537–569). Bethesda, MD: National Association of School Psychologists.

U.S. General Accounting Office. (1994). *Elementary school children: Many change schools frequently, harming their education.* Washington, DC: Author.

Vellutino, F. R., Scanlon, D. M., & Spearing, D. (1995). Semantic and phonological coding in poor and normal readers. *Journal of Experimental Child Psychology, 59*, 76–123.

Wood, D., Halfon, N., Scarlata, D., Newacheck, P., & Nessim, S. (1993). Impact of family relocation on children's growth, development, school function, and behavior. *Journal of the American Medical Association, 270*(11), 1334.

Ysseldyke, J. E., & Christenson, S. L. (1988). Linking assessment to intervention. In J. L. Graden, J. E. Zins, & M. J. Curtis (Eds.), *Alternative educational delivery systems: Enhancing instructional options for all students* (pp. 91–110). Washington, DC: National Association of School Psychologists.

*Authors' Note:* The Bethel School District contributed to this article. Research described in this article was supported by a subcontract from the Oregon Department of Education to the University of Oregon (#8948). The original Oregon Reading First grant was made from the U.S. Department of Education to the Oregon Department of Education (#S357A0020038). Statements do not reflect the positions or policies of these agencies, and no official endorsement by them should be inferred.

**Jean Louise M. Smith** (jsmith@pacificir.org) is a Research Associate at Pacific Institutes for Research in Eugene, Oregon. **Hank Fien** (ffien@uoregon.edu) is a Research Associate at the Center on Teaching and Learning, University of Oregon. **Stan C. Paine** (spaine@rmccorp.com) is the Director of the Western Regional Reading First Technical Assistance Center in Eugene, Oregon.

Originally published in the April 2008 issue of *Educational Leadership*, 65(7): pp. 59–63.

# 8

# The American Dream:
# Slipping Away?

Susan B. Neuman

*Economic inequality is real and growing. It can*
*place low-income and high-income children on*
*separate trajectories throughout school.*

There is a national ethos among Americans that captures our faith in progress, opportunity, and striving. It's the belief that if you work hard and play by the rules, you can succeed and prosper regardless of your original social status or the circumstances of your birth. This American dream has given hope to people born without privilege, and it's one of the main reasons people have often struggled to come to the United States from around the world.

But many people are now beginning to fear that the American dream is slipping away. Economic inequality is real and growing. Between 1977 and 2007, the income of families at the 99th percentile increased by 90 percent; the income of those at the bottom 20th percentile, by just 7 percent (Duncan & Murnane, 2011). Further, the unemployment rate remains dispiritingly high. Especially among those with a high school education or less, the Great Recession wreaked havoc among working-class families' employment (Carnevale & Rose, 2011).

Astonishing increases in the degree of residential segregation are exacerbating these circumstances, according to demographer Douglas Massey (2007). Those with money are more likely to live in homogeneously privileged neighborhoods and interact almost exclusively with other affluent people. Those without money are increasingly confined to homogeneously poor neighborhoods, yielding a density of material deprivation that is unprecedented in U.S. history.

These stark inequalities have become fodder for increasingly intractable debates among politicians and pundits. More important, however, is what these statistics mean for educating our children and keeping the hope of upward mobility through hard work alive. Are there still real opportunities for all children? Or is the American dream now an empty promise?

## Early Experiences and Inequality

On the basis a 10-year study that my colleagues and I conducted of two neighborhoods within the confines of Philadelphia, one of poverty and the other of privilege (Neuman & Celano, 2012), one could argue that our fears are real. Although the dream of upward mobility still exists, it has become far more difficult for many to accomplish.

Our work in these two neighborhoods was guided by the theory that the amount of early access to print and the quality of adult support young children receive set in motion a process that either accelerates or delays literacy development and knowledge acquisition (Stanovich, 1986). Children learn about literacy through experiences and observations of the written language they encounter in their everyday lives. They construct an understanding of how print works through independent explorations of print and signs, interactions around books and other print resources, and participation with others engaged in both enjoyable and purposeful literacy activities. These early experiences provide opportunities to learn about the spelling-to-sound code, build-ing preparatory skills that are essential for learning to read.

Those who are not initiated early on through such environmental print exposure are likely to experience greater difficulty in breaking the spelling-to-sound code. They come to school needing specialized help, and the remediation exercises they receive expose them to less text than the reading exercises that are given to their more skilled peers. They often find themselves working with materials that are too difficult for them to read—or too easy for them to learn from. This combination of difficulties in decoding, lack of practice, and inappropriate materials results in unrewarding early reading experiences. Children struggle to develop fluency in reading, further draining their capacity for compre-hending text.

But it doesn't end there. The vicious cycle accelerates. As the Common Core State Standards emphasize, children gain knowledge through text. Knowledge disparities, therefore, grow as a result of these differences in reading experiences. Those who read more are creating and using greater pools of knowledge. Greater knowledge use enhances students' speed of information acquisition, which over time is likely to accelerate a knowledge gap between those who have access and those who do not (Neuman & Celano, 2006). Although the have-nots gain knowledge, the haves gain it faster. By gaining faster, they gain more. The result, we hypothesized, leads to the social stratification of information capital that occurs among those who live in affluent and poor communities.

Unfortunately, this is what we found.

## Two Neighborhoods

Like many cities throughout the United States, Philadelphia is a city of contrasts. It has become home to many immigrants (Polish, Italian, Irish, Russian, Hispanic, Chinese, and Southeast Asian) and African Americans as a result of industrialization in the late 19th and early

20th centuries. Philadelphia is known as a city of neighborhoods: Its residents live in neat brick row homes as well as back alleys and decaying buildings. Some children in this city will grow up in abject poverty; others, in highly privileged circumstances.

We chose to study two neighborhoods that were representative of these contrasts. Kensington, also known as the Badlands, is a dense, multiethnic community consisting of Puerto Rican, black, Vietnamese, Eastern European, and Caucasian residents with a poverty rate of 90 percent, almost 29 percent unemployment, and approximately 5,000 children under age 17. In contrast, Chestnut Hill is a highly gentrified neighborhood, 80 percent Caucasian and 20 percent black, with a child population of about 1,200. Families there tend to be educated professionals, with the average home costing in the $400,000s. The neighborhood borders several large parks and is somewhat geographically isolated from the rest of the city.

For more than 10 years, we examined how these contrasting ecologies of affluence and poverty might contribute to disparities in reading and the development of information capital (see details in Neuman & Celano, 2012). We engaged in observations, interviews, and activities, using many different analytic tools to understand how these environments might influence children's opportunities for education.

## Stark Differences

### Differences in Print Resources

Right from the beginning, there are differences in the amount and quality of print children in these two neighborhoods are exposed to in their worlds. For example, a 3-year-old in Chestnut Hill would likely see signs with iconic symbols in good readable condition, professionally designed with clear colors and strong graphics. In contrast, many of the signs in the Badlands neighborhood are covered with graffiti with taggers' distinctive signatures, rendering them impossible for a young child to decipher. We found that 74 percent of signs in the Badlands were in poor condition, compared with 1 percent in Chestnut Hill.

The disparities continue when it comes to the availability of print resources appropriate for young children. In Chestnut Hill, we found 11 stores that sold print materials for children, 7 of which even had special sections just for children. In contrast, the Badlands, with a far greater density of children, had only 4 places that carried children's print materials.

Even more troubling were the differences in choices available to a parent selecting a book for a child. Children in Chestnut Hill had access to thousands of book, magazine, and comic book titles, whereas children in the Badlands could access only a small fraction of materials. Our calculations indicated about 13 titles for every child in the community of privilege, and about 1 title for about every 20 children in the community of poverty.

Schools and outside institutions, like the library—often considered safety nets for those who lack resources—did not alter this pattern. In Chestnut Hill preschools, average book condition was excellent, with a wide assortment to choose from; book condition for those in the Badlands was merely adequate, with a limited selection. Differences were even more stark in elementary school libraries. Schools in Chestnut Hill had more than two times the selection of books compared to those in the Badlands. Further, other resources to support children's reading, like computers and trained librarians, were missing in the Badlands.

In short, differences in the economic circumstances of children who live in these neighborhoods translated into extraordinary differences in the availability of print resources.

## Differences in Adult Supports

Material resources represent only one kind of support in creating an environment for reading and the development of information capital.

Even more important is the type of adult support and mentoring that children receive.

In a now-classic study, Annette Lareau (2003) identified parenting practices associated with social class. According to her research, parents from middle- and upper-middle-class families typically engage in a child-rearing strategy known as *concerted cultivation*, consciously developing children's use of language, reasoning skills, and negotiation abilities. In contrast, working-class and poor parents tend to practice—not necessarily by choice—a more hands-off type of child rearing known as *natural growth*. These parents generally have less education and time to impress on their children the values that will give them an advantage in school. Their children often spend less time in the company of adults and more time with other children in self-directed, open-ended play. The differing strategies reinforce class divisions.

Spending hundreds of hours in the public libraries in each neighborhood watching parent–child behaviors, we found a consistent pattern. In the spirit of concerted cultivation, toddlers and preschoolers in Chestnut Hill were carefully guided in selecting appropriate reading materials. Activities were highly focused, with the accompanying adult suggesting books, videos, or audiobooks to check out. The parent clearly appeared to be the arbiter for book selection, noting, "That book is too hard for you," "That is too easy," or "This one might be better."

In contrast, children in the Badlands largely entered the library alone or with a peer, sometimes with a sibling, but rarely with an adult. They would wander in, maybe flip through some pages of a book, and wander out. Without adult assistance, a child would pick up a book, look at the cover, pause for a moment to try to figure it out, and then put it down. Occasionally an older child might help locate a book or read to a younger child. But more often than not, preschooler activity would appear as short bursts, almost frenetic in nature.

To examine how these patterns may influence early reading development, we counted the age of the child, whether the child was accompanied by an adult, and the content and amount of text that might be read to children in each community. We found a disturbing pattern: For every hour we spent observing at the library in Chestnut Hill, more than three-quarters of the time—47 minutes—was spent with an adult reading to a child. During the same time period, not one adult entered the preschool area in the Badlands. By our estimate, children in Chestnut Hill heard nearly 14 times the number of words read in print *per library visit* as children in the Badlands.

## Differences in Independent Reading

We suspected that the early years established a pattern of reading behavior that would affect later development. Consequently, we next focused on the tween years (ages 10–13), when students need to read challenging informational text independently and use self-teaching strategies to learn essential academic vocabulary and concepts.

To examine independent reading, we spent hours in the public library in each neighborhood, recording what students were reading, the average grade level of the text, and whether it was informational or entertainment reading activity. We then conducted a similar analysis of students' use of the computers.

We found an all-too-predictable pattern. Perhaps most alarming was the difference in the challenge level of the texts students selected to read. Students in the Badlands tended to select easy materials. Although 58 percent of the materials read were at grade level, 42 percent were designed for younger children. It was not uncommon to see a 13-year-old boy reading *Highlights* magazine or *Arthur's Eyes*, a book typically favored by the preschool crowd. Challenging words related to academic disciplines are rarely found in these kinds of books and magazines. In contrast, 93 percent of students from Chestnut Hill tended to read at their age level, with a small percentage (7 percent) reading more-challenging above-level materials.

Further, there were striking differences in the amount of time spent reading and the genre of text selected. Students from the Badlands spent considerably less time reading than students from Chestnut

Hill, and the majority of reading time in the Badlands was spent with entertainment materials. A similar pattern occurred with computers and the Internet in the Badlands library: the majority of time was spent watching movies or game-like shows. For students in Chestnut Hill, these patterns were reversed. Most of the students' time was spent on informational texts. In fact, these students spent about 12 times the amount of time on informational reading materials in print and about 5 times more on informational websites than they spent on entertainment content in print and online.

Consequently, by the time students are in their tweens, we see a pattern of reading that leads to a knowledge gap. Reading challenging informational text enhances the speed of information gathering and knowledge acquisition. Reading low-level text of questionable value is likely to keep one at status quo, or worse, be a waste of time. Continued unabated, this gap between the "information haves" and "information have-nots" could lead to even greater social and economic inequality in our society that will be difficult, if not impossible, to reverse.

## Changing the Trajectory

I have painted a bleak picture of the gap between poverty and privilege not to suggest its inevitability but to galvanize people to action. So what can we do? Consider the following steps.

### Un-level the Playing Field

Programs like Title I are based on a policy of "leveling the playing field," ensuring that education resources for poor communities are equal to those for the more affluent. But the notion of providing equal resources is only helpful when none of the competing partners has an advantage at the outset. As we have seen, that is certainly not the case for students who come from poor neighborhoods when compared with more affluent peers.

We need to tip the balance not by equalizing funding but by providing *more* resources and additional supports to students in poor neighborhoods. Not just extra funding, but additional human resources are needed. Training paraprofessionals for such simple activities as reading one-on-one with children in libraries like those in the Badlands could have enormous benefits later on.

## Strengthen Parent Involvement

School programs often profess the importance of parent involvement, but schools rarely offer sustained, intensive parent involvement training programs. We need programs that help parents become the advocates they wish to be by teaching them about the skills and strategies children will need to be successful in school. Such programs will help them make judgments about what kinds of language and literacy experiences to look for in preschool and child-care settings, what to look for in initial reading instruction in kindergarten and the early grades, what to ask principals and other policymakers who make decisions regarding reading instruction, and how to determine whether their child is making adequate progress in reading or needs additional instruction.

## Engage Students' Minds

Far too often, people underestimate the capabilities of students who live in poor neighborhoods, equating poverty with low ability. In reality, however, these students are eager to learn and develop greater expertise when given opportunities to do so.

In public policy, our targets for these students have been to help them graduate from high school and become college-ready. In fact, if students from poor families are to have a fighting chance, they will need far more. They will need a rich knowledge base. They will need to learn how to participate in a new kind of information fabric in which learning, playing, and creative thinking interact in ways that not only use existing knowledge, but also advance it in new directions. We deceive them and ourselves if we expect any less.

## Economically Integrate Schools

Schools today reflect their neighborhoods. Throughout the United States, schools are economically segregated, exacerbating the problems of inequality.

Schools in poor areas struggle for many reasons, but among the most prominent are their rotating faculty of inexperienced teachers and administrators and their low-level curriculum. In contrast, schools in affluent areas are more stable, with more highly trained teachers, rigorous curriculum, fewer discipline problems, and more support from volunteers. Studies have shown that economic integration can begin to change this scenario (Kahlenberg, 2001).

## Reclaiming the Dream

Americans are a resilient people. We remain a formidable force in the knowledge economy. Nevertheless, the last decade's economic chaos and rising inequality has led some to question whether there is a future for the American dream. For those of us who believe that this concept is still what defines us and makes America great, it is time to renew our determination to recapture the American dream and make it a reality for *all* our children.

# References

Carnevale, A., & Rose, S. (2011). *The undereducated American*. Washington, DC: Georgetown Center on Education and the Workforce.

Duncan, G., & Murnane, R. (Eds.). (2011). *Whither opportunity?* New York: Russell Sage Foundation.

Kahlenberg, R. (2001). *All together now*. Washington, DC: Brookings.

Lareau, A. (2003). *Unequal childhoods*. Berkeley: University of California Press.

Massey, D. (2007). *Categorically unequal*. New York: Russell Sage Foundation.

Neuman, S. B., & Celano, D. (2006). The knowledge gap: Implications of leveling the playing field for low-income and middle-income children. *Reading Research Quarterly, 41*, 176–201.

Neuman, S. B., & Celano, D. (2012). *Giving our children a fighting chance: Affluence, literacy, and the development of information capital.* New York: Teachers College Press.

Stanovich, K. E. (1986). Matthew effects in reading: Some consequences of individual differences in the acquisition of literacy. *Reading Research Quarterly, 21*, 360–406.

**Susan B. Neuman** (sbneuman@umich.edu) is a professor in Educational Studies at the University of Michigan in Ann Arbor and professor of Teaching and Learning at New York University. She is the author, with Donna Celano, of *Giving Our Children a Fighting Chance: Affluence, Literacy, and the Development of Information Capital* (Teachers College Press, 2012).

Originally published in the May 2013 issue of *Educational Leadership, 70*(8): pp. 18–22.

## 9

# Think Big, Bigger ... and Smaller

Richard E. Nisbett

*When it comes to closing achievement gaps, big
interventions are not always big enough—and small
interventions can yield surprising results.*

Few questions in education are more pressing than this one: How can
we reduce academic achievement gaps between middle-class and poor
children and between white children and children of color? The class
and ethnicity gaps are significant for all types of testing, including those
for academic skills and IQ.

Almost a decade ago, the U.S. Congress passed the No Child
Left Behind Act, which directed schools to eliminate the gaps in
standardized test scores by 2014. I don't know whether the act was
passed in the cynical knowledge that no such massive change could
be accomplished so quickly or in the naive belief that sheer will and a
little money would suffice to achieve it. In any case, we clearly won't
make the deadline.

The barriers to reducing the gaps are large. In fact, it's doubtful
that we can ever bring the social class gap to zero; people with more
money are always going to see to it that their children get more and

better education than the children of people with less money. The gaps among black, Hispanic, and white children can doubtless be greatly reduced in the short term and completely eliminated in the long run. But the root causes of gaps are complex, and the class and ethnicity gaps are intertwined.

I am a social psychologist, and two important general principles in my field are (1) some big-seeming interventions have little or no effect, and (2) some small-seeming interventions have significant effects. Both of these principles are confirmed over and over again in the field of education.

## Preschool Interventions: Big and Bigger

Head Start seems like a big intervention. It's certainly expensive. It places poor and minority children in settings designed to provide developmental support and at least some intellectually stimulating activities. But Head Start's academic effects are slight—reduction of the gap by a few IQ points at the beginning of elementary school, which fades into nothing after a few years of school. The effect on grades is similarly transient (Ludwig & Miller, 2005).

Fortunately, there are bigger preschool interventions that do have marked effects on closing academic achievement gaps. An example is the High/Scope Perry Preschool program serving low-income black children in Ypsilanti, Michigan. This program provided two and one-half hours of quality preschool instruction each weekday from October through May to children at ages 3 and 4. Most of the activities were deliberately chosen to increase intelligence and academic skills, and teachers made weekly home visits to each child's family (Schweinhart, 2003). Another program, the Abecedarian Project, provided even more intense intervention. Participants received a full-day, year-round program with a low child–teacher ratio from infancy through age 5 (Campbell et al., 2001).

Both of these programs employed educators with considerable skill and experience—criteria that Head Start often fails to meet. The souped-up programs resulted in big IQ gains on entry into elementary school and massive academic gains that persisted for the long haul. Just how massive were these gains? The programs cut in half the percentage of children who were put into special education, cut by almost two-thirds the percentage who scored in the bottom 10 percent on standardized tests, reduced by almost one-half the percentage who had to repeat a grade, increased by one-third the percentage who graduated from high school, more than doubled the percentage who went to a four-year college, and cut in half the percentage who were on welfare as adults. The programs were expensive, but the payoff to the public has been estimated at $4–$9 per dollar spent.

So although some big-seeming measures may fail, experience shows that if you really knock yourself out, you can produce enormous effects.

## K–12 Interventions: Big and Bigger

We also see some big-seeming interventions in K–12 schools that have produced disappointing results. For example, vouchers sound like a big intervention to many people. You give families money that will pay for education at any school in the community. This arrangement is supposed to match students to the schools that are best for them and either improve or eliminate the least-effective schools as parents begin to shun them. But there is no evidence that vouchers result in better scholastic outcomes for kids (Rothstein, 2004).

How about charter schools? They can design their own programs and hire and fire teachers without necessarily having to deal with unions. But the best evidence we have indicates that most charters are little better than regular public schools, and perhaps slightly worse during their start-up periods (Gleason, Clark, Tuttle, & Dwoyer, 2010).

So-called "whole school" interventions sound ambitious. Corporations go into a school with a new curriculum, lesson plans, special teacher training, reorganization of the administration, and so on. But there's not much evidence that they improve things (Rothstein, 2004). Schools undergoing such makeovers are often only a little improved by the experience—and such interventions are very expensive, so the bang for the buck is poor.

But again, some *really* big K–12 interventions do make a huge difference for poor and minority kids. Uncommon Schools, Achievement First, Harlem Children's Zone, and KIPP (Knowledge Is Power Program) provide as much as 60 percent more time in school than regular public schools do.

In the best-researched program, KIPP, students start as early as 7:30 a.m. and stay as late as 5:00 p.m., attend school on some Saturdays, and continue into the summer for a few weeks. Kids get experiences that are typical of what upper-middle-class children get—museums, sports, dance, art, theater, photography, and music lessons. Teachers visit parents and children in their homes, insist on kindness and civility, and hand out rewards on the spot for good behavior and academic achievement. One KIPP teacher described the atmosphere:

> We've never had a kid talk back to a teacher, and we've never had kids fight. I don't attribute this to the discipline system. It's from setting expectations from the start. ... It's because kids believe that this is an extraordinary place, and we've taught them that. I don't think they don't tease because they are afraid of the bench (for bad behavior). It's just something that they would not do at KIPP. This is the one school they've been to where there's no teasing. They feel safe, and they are learning more. (David et al., 2006, p. 16)

And KIPP gets results. A Stanford Research Institute study found that students who entered 5th grade in KIPP schools in the San Francisco

Bay area achieved marked improvement in a year. The proportion of students scoring at or above average on a nationally standardized language arts test rose from 25 percent at the beginning of the school year to 44 percent in the spring. In math, the proportion was 37 percent in the fall and 65 percent in the spring. Progress continued at a good clip through middle school (David et al., 2006).

Again, big-seeming interventions sometimes fail to have big effects, but *really* big interventions can have huge effects.

How about high school? There are no KIPP-type programs for high school yet, but we do have a pretty good idea of what can be achieved with poor minority students in math. You may have seen *Stand and Deliver*, the movie about math teacher Jaime Escalante's achievement in getting his East Los Angeles barrio students to pass advanced placement (AP) calculus at higher rates than students in most elite U.S. high schools. But is the story true?

There's good news and bad news about Escalante's feat. It's perfectly true that it happened. But it didn't happen in the way the movie implies. Escalante didn't just suddenly announce to unsuspecting seniors that he was going to make them into math whizzes that year. He built up math programs at junior high feeder schools, which brought highly prepared students into his three-year high school. Then, he made sure his students had excellent courses in high school math before he ever got them as seniors (Jessness, 2002). Once again, ambitious interventions can make a real difference.

## The Potential of Thinking Small

I started out by saying that big interventions don't always have big effects, but small interventions *can* have big effects. That's decidedly true for small interventions that address ethnic achievement gaps.

For example, social psychologist Carol Dweck found, not surprisingly, that students who believe that ability is a matter of hard work get higher grades than students who believe that ability is fixed from birth. Dweck and her colleagues taught a group of low-income, minority students that learning forms neural connections and changes the brain and that students are in charge of this process. Dweck reports that some tough junior high school boys were actually reduced to tears by the news that their intelligence was substantially under their own control. Students exposed to the intervention worked harder, according to their teachers, and got higher grades than students in a control condition. The intervention was more effective for students who initially believed that intelligence was a matter of genes than it was for students who already tended to believe it was a matter of hard work (Dweck, 2007).

Aronson, Fried, and Good (2002) performed similar experiments, with dramatic results. They conducted one study with low-income, minority students in Texas who were entering junior high school. The intervention was short and simple. For the first year of junior high, each student was assigned a college-student mentor who helped him or her explore a variety of issues related to school adjustment.

The mentors for the control group gave their mentees information about drugs and encouraged their mentees to avoid taking them. The mentors for the experimental group told their mentees about the expandable nature of intelligence and how the brain can make new connections throughout life. Students in each group were introduced to a website that reinforced their mentors' message; the experimental group website included animated illustrations of how the brain forms new connections when it solves new problems. The mentors also helped the students design a web page in which they presented this message through words and pictures of their own making.

The effects of the intervention were dramatic. On the Texas Assessment of Academic Skills (TAAS) in math, the performance of male students exposed to the intervention was much higher than that of males not exposed to the intervention; for females, the difference was even larger. Students exposed to the intervention also did much better on the TAAS reading test than did students in the control group.

Oyserman, Bybee, and Terry (2006) set up an easy-to-pull-off intervention with low-income students in a largely black and Hispanic junior high school. The students attended several sessions designed to make them think about what kind of future they wanted to have, what difficulties they might encounter along the way, how they could deal with those difficulties, and which of their friends could help them. These sessions were supplemented with others in which students worked in small groups, exploring how to deal with everyday problems, social difficulties, academic challenges, and the process of getting to high school graduation. The intervention had a modest effect on grade point average (enough to take a student from the 40th percentile to the 50th percentile); a bigger effect on standardized test scores (enough to take a student from the 35th percentile to the 50th percentile); and reduced by more than one-half the likelihood of being retained in grade.

One small intervention with students in a racially mixed high school had breathtakingly large effects. Cohen, Garcia, Apfel, and Master (2006) asked students just beginning high school to write about their most important values—sports, school achievement, family, and so on. This activity had no effect on white students or high-performing black students. But it had a huge effect on low-performing black students, substantially improving their grade point averages and reducing the need for remediation from 18 percent to 5 percent. The researchers reasoned that the exercise was self-affirming, building students' confidence, making them feel more a part of things and more comfortable in their surroundings, and helping them overcome stereotype threat (performance-inhibiting anxiety about being judged on the basis of negative stereotypes). Interestingly, the same intervention had no effect on black students in a racially segregated school, where stereotype threat would assumedly be less of a factor.

Small interventions can also make a difference in college. Most new college students worry about social acceptance and fitting in on campus, but this can be particularly worrisome for black and Hispanic students. Walton and Cohen (2007) performed a modest intervention to address race-based doubts about belonging among black students at a prestigious private university. They invited 18 black and 19 white freshmen to review the results of a survey of older students at their school, which revealed that worries about social acceptance were common among students of all races and that most students eventually found a comfortable social niche.

The intervention had no effect on white students, but it had a big positive effect on black students. Following the intervention, the black students reported studying more, making more contacts with professors, and attending more review sessions and study group meetings. During the subsequent term, the black students in the intervention group earned much higher grades than the black students in the control group did.

## What Will It Take?

We know that much can be done from infancy through college to reduce the achievement gap. We also know that some expensive and big-seeming interventions have little effect, whereas some even more expensive interventions can have huge effects.

How much more expensive? If we put the poorest one-sixth of elementary school students in KIPP-type programs, that would cost about $18 billion dollars a year. (Current KIPP-type programs cost little more than regular public schools, but that's only because their teachers work about 60 percent more than regular public school teachers for only slightly higher pay. We clearly can't duplicate that on a large scale.) If we put the poorest one-sixth of young children into highly effective preschool programs, the cost would be about $50 billion a year. Both of these moves would be good investments if we're really serious about equalizing educational opportunity and outcomes.

Can we afford this kind of outlay for education for the poor? Well, Congress felt in 2001 that we could afford $130 billion a year in tax cuts for the richest one percent of Americans. And the bill for bailing out AIG was $145 billion dollars.

Bear in mind that some very big-seeming interventions don't cost much more than school as usual. Jaime Escalante's enriched math classes are one example. And of course, the small-seeming interventions with notable effects discussed here cost next to nothing.

So when it comes to reducing the achievement gap, don't think big. Think *very* big … and very small.

## References

Aronson, J., Fried, C. B., & Good, C. (2002). Reducing stereotype threat and boosting academic achievement of African-American students: The role of conceptions of intelligence. *Journal of Experimental Social Psychology, 38,* 113–125.

Campbell, F. A., Pungello, E. P., Miller-Johnson, S., Burchinal, M., et al. (2001). The development of cognitive and academic abilities: Growth curves from an early childhood educational experiment. *Developmental Psychology, 37,* 231–242.

Cohen, G. L., Garcia, J., Apfel, N., & Master, A. (2006). Reducing the racial achievement gap: A social-psychological intervention. *Science, 313,* 1307–1310.

David, J. L., Woodworth, K., Grant, E., Guha, R., Lopez-Torkos, A., & Young, V. M. (2006). *Bay area KIPP schools: A study of early implementation (First-year report 2004–05).* Menlo Park, CA: SRI International.

Dweck, C. S. (2007). The perils and promise of praise. *Educational Leadership, 65*(2), 34–39.

Gleason, P., Clark, M., Tuttle, C. C., & Dwoyer, E. (2010). *The evaluation of charter school impacts: Final report.* Washington, DC: U.S. Department of Education. Retrieved from http://ies.ed.gov/ncee/pubs/20104029/pdf/20104029.pdf

Jessness, J. (2002). Stand and Deliver revisited. *Reason.* Retrieved from www.reason.com/news/show/28479.html

Ludwig, J., & Miller, D. L. (2005). *Does Head Start improve children's life chances? Evidence from a regression discontinuity design* (Working Paper 11702). Cambridge, MA: National Bureau of Economic Research.

Oyserman, D., Bybee, T., & Terry, K. (2006). Possible selves and academic outcomes: How and when possible selves impel action. *Journal of Personality and Social Psychology, 91,* 188–204.

Rothstein, R. (2004). *Class and schools: Using social, economic, and educational reform to close the black-white achievement gap.* Washington, DC: Economic Policy Institute.

Schweinhart, L. J. (2003, April). *Benefits, costs, and explanation of the High/ Scope Perry Preschool Program.* Paper presented at the Society for Research in Child Development meeting, Tampa, Florida.

Walton, G. M., & Cohen, G. L. (2007). A question of belonging: Race, social fit, and achievement. *Journal of Personality and Social Psychology, 92,* 82–96.

**Richard E. Nisbett** (Nisbett@umich.edu) is distinguished university professor at the University of Michigan, Ann Arbor. He is the author of *Intelligence and How to Get It: Why Schools and Cultures Count* (W.W. Norton, 2009).

Originally published in the November 2010 issue of *Educational Leadership, 68*(3): pp. 10–15.

# 10

# Students Without Homes

Vicky S. Dill

*For students who are struggling with homelessness,
caring educators can make all the difference.*

Jazeke customarily sits at the second lab table in my sophomore physics class, his slender elbows resting lightly on the cool black tabletop.
Covertly intrigued by any science that's "cool," Jazeke can often be
seen arranging the motion sensors, data charts, and chemical rocket
components neatly in the middle of the table. Rolling up the bright
orange sleeves of his Abercrombie and Fitch shirt, he frequently throws
me that "don't call on me, but do" look. I must admit, he's one of my
favorite students.

But this week, Jazeke appears distracted. Homework assignments
are missing. He strains to concentrate, and dark circles deepen under
his eyes. I notice he blows off his best friend, Franklin, when asked,
"Wassup, man?" Something furtive is creeping into his body language.
By week's end, even his upscale woman-magnet hygiene slips.

As the teacher of such a promising science student, I am tempted
to give him a whispered wake-up call, "Jazeke! No one does lazy in my

class!" Instead, I ask him to stay a minute after class. "What's going on? Is something bothering you?"

Long pause. "Yes, miss. But you can't tell nobody." Jazeke's father was laid off five months ago; they were upside down on their mortgage. Last week, Jazeke lived in a middle-class neighborhood; this week he lives in a shelter. Because he's 16, he and his father had to go to one shelter while his mother and sisters went to another. He misses his mom, with whom he's quite close, and their 8-year-old dalmatian, Rumpus, who had to be dropped off at the animal shelter.

Jazeke falls silent, clearly numb. I am quiet, too. Grateful that I muffled my imagined "wake-up call," I can only admire the courage it took for Jazeke to share the truth.

Now I can't help wondering: Is there any way I can help this student whose once luminous eyes are now glazed over and who is intent on hiding from even his best friend the greatest tragedy of his young life thus far?

## Faces of Homelessness

Jazeke mightily shatters the traditional image of homelessness. Put six pictures around the room on the walls: a grandmother and granddaughter, a teenager asleep on a park bench, two parents and their six children outside a mobile home, a 10-year-old sleeping on a couch, a father and his newborn, and a wizened man pushing a cart full of plastic bags. Ask teachers and principals to stand under the picture of someone most likely to be homeless. Crowds will gather under the man with the cart.

Most educators are only gradually awakening to the fact that many of their students may not have homes. In fact, approximately 40 percent of the 3.5 million homeless Americans—between 1.4 and 1.5 million—are children (National Law Center on Homelessness and

Poverty, 2009). Further, data suggest that one in 50 U.S. children experiences homelessness in any given year (National Center on Family Homelessness, 2009). These children—pushed out of their homes as a result of economic hardship, foreclosure, eviction, or abuse—may be in any classroom, in any row, at any lab table. Younger children are more likely to talk about their difficult living situation, but for students in upper elementary and beyond, the stigma is harsh.

It's understandable that most educators are not fully aware of the prevalence and signs of homelessness or the federal laws that have been in effect since 1987 to protect homeless students. Few certification programs delve into significant detail about how to identify or help students in unstable or homeless situations. So if teachers or principals learn that one of their students has recently become homeless, what can they do?

## The Liaison: A Crucial Role

The Stewart B. McKinney Homeless Assistance Act, signed into law by President Ronald Reagan in 1987 and last reauthorized and amended as the McKinney-Vento law in 2001 (Project Hope-Virginia, 2009), requires every school district to appoint a homeless liaison. Ideally, the liaison is a highly trained advocate who is thoroughly familiar with the law's requirements (see Figure 10.1) and who works to creatively facilitate homeless students' academic and social success.

"When I came to this district three years ago," says Nancy, director of federal programs at a suburban school district, "they told me we didn't have any homeless students. I asked what we would do if one of our kids did become homeless, and they said we would refer them to the homeless liaison. 'Who is that?' I asked. 'Well, I guess that would be you.'"

After Nancy received training in the definition of homelessness, she discovered that some 55 students in the district were, in fact, homeless.

## Figure 10.1: What Are the Rights of Homeless Children?

Students in homeless situations have the right to

- Be identified as homeless and receive Title I services and other supports to ensure their academic success.
- Be immediately enrolled in school despite their unstable housing situation and despite their inability to produce documents ordinarily required of students who have a permanent residence.
- Receive assistance in procuring school records.
- Be allowed to stay in the school they attended when they became homeless or the school in which they were last enrolled (called school of origin).
- Be transported from their current place of residence to the school of origin to reduce the need for them to transfer from school to school.
- Receive free school nutrition.
- Receive referrals to medical, mental health, dental, and other appropriate services.
- Receive assistance in acquiring school supplies, standard dress or uniforms, backpacks, and other provisions needed to succeed in school.

Source: *McKinney-Vento Homeless Assistance Act.* Retrieved from National Center for Homeless Education at http://center.serve.org/nche/downloads/mv_full_text.pdf

The backgrounds or preparation of the individuals who fill the role of homeless liaison vary greatly from school district to school district. Large districts with many homeless students may have one or more full-time liaisons; smaller districts usually fold this responsibility into other positions, such as Title I director, director of federal programs, director of counseling, grants director, assistant superintendent, or principal.

It is the liaison's job to keep teachers, counselors, and front-office personnel informed about the law. At times, registrars and school administrative assistants may hold a family's very future in their hands, as was the case for the Bourgeois family.

When the Bourgeois family fled Hurricane Katrina, registrars in the first two districts they approached refused to enroll their three children because they couldn't show birth certificates, school records, immunization papers, or, in one case, proof of residency. After the third school district refused admission, 16-year-old Tiara dropped out and got a fast-food job. At long last, when the family reached their cousin's house in Tennessee and settled in to regroup, they encountered a front-office staff that was well informed and who welcomed the family warmly regardless of their ability to show records.

The liaison also collaborates with registrars to systematically query students regarding their living situation, using a form sometimes called a *residency questionnaire*. Carefully worded to avoid the term *homeless*, these questionnaires are routinely gathered at the beginning of each year. Registrars notify the liaison about responses that indicate students may not have a stable residence.

Despite systematic efforts, however, underidentification of homeless students is widespread. Because of the stigma of homelessness, families may not fill in questionnaires accurately. Parents may feel that they have failed their children if they admit that their housing is unstable. Victims of abuse may be afraid to share their residence information. Teens on their own may not want their parents to find them. For numerous reasons, homeless students often are not recognized and do not receive the services they desperately need.

## Identifying Homeless Students

Under the McKinney-Vento law, children who lack a "fixed, regular, and adequate" residence are considered homeless. Children living in parks, bus stations, cars, shelters, abandoned or foreclosed buildings, and so on are relatively easy to identify as homeless. What educators sometimes miss is that the law's definition also includes "children and youth who are sharing the housing of other persons due to loss of housing, economic hardship, or similar reason" (National Center for Homeless Education, n.d.). Trinity Byers is an example of such a student.

When Trinity ran away from her abusive stepfather to live with her aunt in an adjacent district, she struggled to find rides back and forth to Lombardi High. She was frequently tardy or absent. Her grades fell; she become petulant and moody. Afraid that she might fail a grade, her aunt suggested that Trinity go to the high school just down the street, but Trinity was adamant about not losing her friends. Her fear was so overwhelming that she wrote about it in her daily English class journal.

When Trinity's English teacher became aware of her struggle, he contacted the school counselor (who was also the homeless liaison) to see whether anything could be done. Fortunately, the law provides transportation for homeless students to the school of origin—the school the student was attending when he or she became homeless. Identifying Trinity as homeless made a fundamental difference in her future. Now that Trinity was assured of a ride to and from school every day, her attendance picked up. She kept her friends and was promoted to the next grade.

Thus, the caring detective radar of every teacher is an indispensable tool for identifying homeless students in preK–12 schools. Students frequently become homeless midyear or between distributions of residency questionnaires. Teachers may overhear students discussing the fact that they are "couch-surfing." More crucially, if teachers observe the following signs, they should consider the possibility that a student has become homeless.

## Depression

Students who become homeless experience many personal losses and endure jarring conditions. They often have a tremendous fear of changing schools and losing their friends. In a shelter or doubled-up setting, they may encounter crowded conditions and lack an appropriate space to do homework. Food may be unfamiliar, available only during certain

---

**Figure 10.2: What Can Teachers Do?**

- Be sensitive to the possibility that students in your classroom may be homeless.
- If you sense that a student may be in such a situation, contact the district's homeless liaison.
- Be available for conversation if the student wishes to confide in you, but don't push the student into conversation on the topic.
- If you assign homework requiring supplies or materials, ensure that all students have access to needed items; ask the homeless liaison to help.
- Discuss readings, stories, news articles, movies, or literature that explores economic hardship, families without homes, or characters who are resilient; assign writing activities that include these topics as options.
- Do a homelessness awareness activity, such as gathering food, hygiene items, or school supplies for others.
- Create an atmosphere of community in the classroom in which all students' feelings and situations are accepted and stigmatization is out of the question.

---

hours, or scarce; roommates may be incompatible. Prized possessions, such as a teddy bear, game player, or CD collection, may be lost or stolen. Pets, often an emotional anchor in a child's life, may have to be given up. There seems to be little to hold onto.

Students who do not normally display the symptoms of depression but suddenly become listless, pessimistic, or jaded may have become homeless. For students with unstable housing who frequently move in and out of homelessness, each move adds a measure of disorientation and anxiety that may rapidly become chronic.

Students from 11 to 17 years old who are homeless or highly mobile are twice as likely to commit suicide as students with stable housing. If the family moves more than 10 times, children are four times more likely to attempt suicide than those who never moved (Qin, Mortensen, & Pederson, 2009). For students who are highly mobile or homeless, counseling and therapy are not luxuries, but crucial tools for mental health in a bleak and seemingly endless cycle.

## Poor Health, Hygiene, and Nutrition

Other signals that a student may be homeless include an escalation in colds, asthma, allergies, rashes, or other illnesses that threaten regular attendance and concentration. Seldom will a homeless student have a doctor's excuse for absences; health care is rare among students experiencing homelessness. Students who normally exhibit excellent self-care may now arrive in class with rumpled clothing and poor hygiene, or they may wear the same outfit over and over. They may hoard food in their backpacks or sneak it in class.

## Chronic Stress

High levels of anxiety and stress are to be expected in both chronically and newly homeless students. Students may be unable to concentrate or memorize; they may fall asleep in class. Chronic stress affects the executive function of the brain, so students may be unable to plan projects, keep materials organized, pay attention, negotiate unexpected events in the classroom, or control their emotions. They may be unable to trust anyone, thinking that their secret is about to be disclosed and feeling that they are no longer in control of their lives.

Students' body language may become quite defensive, exuding a pervasive sense of loss and panic. Anger and fear of discovery may lead to lying, aggression, or withdrawal. Sadly, economic hardship may preclude participation in some of the activities that students could use for stress relief. Participation in sports, band and orchestra, or school clubs may no longer be possible because transportation to school events and resources for uniforms, instrument rental, or field trips have disappeared. Students may become loners—a response that may be exacerbated by bullying over their poor hygiene, dirty clothes, and unconventional living situation.

## The Power to Make a Difference

Being homeless does not mean being hopeless. When school personnel are sensitive and supportive, school can be a place where students in homeless situations receive much-needed structure, reliable relationships, physical and emotional nurture, and motivation.

Teachers can start by being aware that when unusual discipline issues erupt, they may be symptoms of a deeper problem. Caution is always in order; escalating conflict with a child who is struggling with homelessness ("What's wrong with you, young lady? You never bring in your homework!") can bring about a devastating moment in a young life. Abusive behavior, such as peer bullying, humiliation, or sarcasm toward homeless youth, must be calmly and firmly eliminated from the classroom.

In terms of instruction, teachers can use strategies that work well for students under stress, such as active participation, teamwork, investigative learning, community building, hands-on projects, and so on. Teachers who know about a student's living situation should also remember that it's difficult to complete homework in a shelter. Shelters are often noisy; inevitably, there are lights-out times; there is little space to complete assignments; and computers are often unavailable or broken. Children living in shelters, outdoors, in cars, or in doubled-up situations frequently lose backpacks, calculators, pens, and books to theft.

Teachers should be cautious about "draw your home" assignments that would require students to either go underground about their situation or risk being stigmatized. Caution is also in order when assignments require outside equipment or materials; if students have not been identified and assisted, they may not have the resources to buy supplies for school projects, go on field trips, or travel to peers' homes to complete assignments.

Teachers who suspect that a student may be homeless can contribute tremendously to his or her well-being by having a simple conversation. Teachers should avoid using the word *homeless*, but should instead ask whether the student is experiencing some transition or change. Is anything going on that the student is willing to share? Would the student like an opportunity to talk to someone about these changes?

If the teacher confirms that the student may be homeless, he or she should contact the homeless liaison, who can quietly make helpful resources available. For high school students especially, identification can be a life-changing improvement; for example, scholarships and significant assistance through financial aid have recently become available (see National Association for the Education of Homeless Children and Youth, 2009).

Homeless students may feel they have little to look forward to as they face the daily struggle of finding a decent place to sleep, food to eat, and a sense of stability. But aware and caring teachers have the power to build an emotional home in the classroom and, as many do every day, save the life and future of a child.

## References

National Association for the Education of Homeless Children and Youth (2009). *Setting the context*. Retrieved from www.naehcy.org/higher_ed.html

National Center on Family Homelessness. (2009). *America's youngest outcasts: State report card on child homelessness*. Newton, MA: Author. Retrieved fromwww.homelesschildrenamerica.org/report.php

National Center for Homeless Education. (n.d.). *McKinney-Vento definition of homelessness*. Retrieved from http://center.serve.org/nche/definition.php

National Law Center on Homelessness and Poverty. (2009). *Key data concerning homeless children and youth*. Retrieved from www.nlchp.org/program_fact sheets.cfm?prog=2

Project Hope-Virginia (2009). *History of the McKinney Act*. Williamsburg, VA: College of William and Mary, School of Education. Retrieved from http://education.wm.edu/centers/hope/resources/mckinneyact/index.php

Qin P., Mortensen, P. B., & Pederson, C. B. (2009). Frequent change of residence and risk of attempted and completed suicide among children and adolescents. *Archives of General Psychiatry, 66*(6), 628–632.

*Author's note:* Names are pseudonyms.

**Vicky S. Dill** ( vickydill@austin.utexas.edu) is senior program coordinator, The Homeless Education Office, Charles A. Dana Center, University of Texas at Austin.

Originally published in the November 2010 issue of *Educational Leadership, 68*(3): pp. 43–47.

# Got Books?

Anne McGill-Franzen and Richard Allington

*A new study suggests that increasing summer reading can help prevent low-income children from losing ground during vacation.*

When Devon started 3rd grade as a new transfer student at inner-city Jefferson Elementary School,[1] he was reading at a 1st grade level. A quiet boy with a shy smile, he appeared eager to try. But he struggled with the sounds of letters and became confused and frustrated when invited to read aloud. Fortunately, Jefferson's dedicated staff had put comprehensive supports in place to help students like Devon. With accurate and frequent assessments to pinpoint his strengths and weaknesses, exposure to rich and varied reading materials, after-school tutoring, and targeted instruction to develop early reading strategies, Devon gained confidence and was almost on grade level by the end of school in June. His teachers, resource specialists, and tutors believed that he was on track to academic success.

Imagine their dismay the following September when Devon, now entering 4th grade, seemed to have forgotten many of his hard-won skills. Beginning-of-the-year assessments placed him back in the lowest reading group, and the round of interventions began again. But this year, Devon felt less hopeful.

Sadly, Devon is typical of many low-income students who make great strides during the school year only to see their gains slip away over the summer break. Their teachers, who might work heroically to help them succeed, are often unfairly blamed for the stubborn achievement gap between these students and their wealthier peers.

## Access to Books Is the Key

Although education policymakers have done little to address this problem, a long history of research has shown that summer reading setback is a primary source of the reading achievement gap. For example, both Hayes and Grether (1983) and, more recently, Alexander, Entwisle, and Olson (2007) reported that summer setback explains approximately 80 percent of the reading achievement gap between poor and nonpoor students at age 14.

Other researchers have examined the factors that contribute to summer setback and have found that it can largely be explained by the lack of summer reading activity. As Heyns (1978) reported, "The single summer activity that is most strongly and consistently related to summer learning is reading" (p. 161). More recently, Kim (2004) found that summer reading activity stemmed summer setback in a sample of 6th grade students in an urban school system.

Students from low-income families are likely to have more restricted access to reading material at home than their more-advantaged peers do. Research confirms enormous discrepancies in the numbers of books in the homes of poor and nonpoor children (Constantino, 2005; Fryer & Levitt, 2002; Neuman, Celano, Greco, & Shue, 2001). Neuman and Celano (2001) found roughly 10 times greater access to reading material in higher-income neighborhoods than in lower-income neighborhoods in the same large urban center.

Research supports the commonsense notion that easier access to interesting reading materials increases the likelihood that people will read. Both Kim (2004) and McQuillan and Au (2001), for example, found that easy availability of reading material strongly predicts the amount of reading activity.

## More Research Evidence

Increasing low-income students' access to books during the summer months seems likely to stimulate reading activity and thereby minimize summer reading loss. Heyns (1978) first raised this hypothesis when she wrote, "the unique contribution of reading to summer learning suggests that increasing access to books and encouraging reading may well have a substantial impact on achievement" (p. 172). In the 30 years since then, however, this idea has received little attention from researchers or policymakers.

Recently, two large-scale randomized field experiments have supported the hypotheses that (1) providing low-income students with easy access to appropriate books would increase the amount of summer reading and (2) increasing the amount of reading would ameliorate summer reading setback. First, Kim (2006) reported on a single summer intervention that provided 252 randomly selected low-income 4th graders in 10 schools with books to read during the summer months. Each student received eight books, which were mailed to him or her every other week during July and August along with a postcard encouraging the student to practice reading both out loud and silently. The students' teachers also instructed them in comprehension strategies and paired reading during the last two weeks of school. The study found small positive effects on reading achievement as measured by the Iowa Tests of Basic Skills when these students were compared with a control group. Gains were especially evident among African American students.

From 2001 to 2004, we conducted a similar study but with a larger sample of students and a longitudinal design (Allington et al., 2007). We provided 12 paperback books each summer to 842 randomly selected primary-grade students eligible for free or reduced-price meals in 17 high-poverty elementary schools. The books were self-selected by the students at book fairs we organized over three consecutive years.

Although the students were overwhelmingly African American, they generally chose books that reflected everyday popular culture rather than books related to African American issues. The top choices of both boys and girls were related to the media—*Hangin' with Hilary Duff, Hangin' with Lil' Romeo*, and so on. The Captain Underpants series was also popular. When students did select literature representing the experiences of African Americans, they reported doing so because their teachers had earlier introduced the book to them.

On the final day of school each year, the students were given the books they had selected. We asked the students to keep a book log and return it at the end of the summer (although few did so).

After three years of participation, we compared the reading achievement (as measured by scores on Florida's Comprehensive Assessment Test) of the experimental group with a control group of 428 low-income students from the same schools who received no books. We found that the reading achievement of the students who received the summer books for three years was significantly higher ($p = .015$) than that of the control-group students. We calculated an overall reading achievement effect size of .14, which was statistically significant, and a slightly larger effect size (ES = .21) for the poorest students. Both of these effect sizes are small. However, both are equivalent to or larger than the effect size Cooper, Nye, Charlton, Lindsay, and Greathouse (1996) reported for attending summer school (ES = .14) and equal to or larger than the achievement effect sizes Borman, Hewes, Overman, and Brown (2003) reported for implementing comprehensive school reform models (ES = .09–.14). Our intervention was less expensive and less extensive than either providing summer school or engaging in comprehensive school reform.

In addition to the positive effects of reading achievement, the students also told us that they liked the opportunity to select their own books at the book fair. Sean, a 3rd grader, told us, "I think the book fair was great. I like it when we pick our own books to read. 'Cause some books other people pick, when you start reading, it's stupid." If we want students to read voluntarily, then offering them the opportunity to select the books seems to be a crucial factor.

We also received some input from parents in the form of written notes in the book logs that we asked students to return. Sometimes parents noted that the books seemed easy or hard or that the students and their siblings appreciated receiving them. Although we rarely got more than a sentence or two from parents or students, there were exceptions. For instance, one mother wrote about Ruby Bridges's book *Through My Eyes*, a firsthand account of early school desegregation,

> My son didn't want to read this book. I started reading the book. It didn't hold his attention. But later he asked me some questions. "What is racism? Are we African Americans? Mom, why did they write a story about Ruby Bridges and who is she?" We are going to keep this book on our bookshelf so every year we can pull it out and read it again and have a discussion on it. So the older they get the more they will be able to understand civil rights and other topics, and why Ruby Bridges's life story was important.

## Getting Books into Students' Hands

To become skilled at almost any activity requires extensive and continual practice, whether the skills are physical or cognitive in nature. Just as an athlete's performance diminishes during the off-season if he or she practices less, students' reading performance falls off during the summer months if they don't read.

These two studies strongly suggest one way to begin to address the long-standing reading achievement gap between low-income students and their more-affluent peers. Too many students, especially poor students, spend their summers with restricted access to books that might engage them in reading. Although many aspects of the way students spend their summer breaks are beyond the control of schools, we can do something about the lack of access to reading materials if we have the will to do so. For example, schools might

- Rethink access to school book collections. School libraries are typically the largest and nearest supply of age-appropriate books for low-income students, but in too many cases there is no access to school and classroom libraries during summer vacation.
- Revisit the school budget to create programs similar to our experimental intervention, routinely sending students home for the summer with a collection of self-selected books.
- Acknowledge the role of popular culture in students' lives. Rather than denigrating series books or books that derive from movies or video games, build on this prior knowledge to create communities of readers who share, discuss, and swap favorite books.
- Identify local knowledge. Children and families in particular communities know a lot about some animals or habitats. For example, our informational books in Florida focused on alligators and swamps in one community and sharks and oceans in another, building on students' interests and background knowledge.

We must create ways to put books into all students' hands during the summer months—and other school vacation periods as well. Ensuring that books are available to any child at any time of the year will be a good first step in enhancing the reading achievement of low-income students and an absolutely necessary step in closing the reading achievement gap.

## Endnote

[1] School and student names are pseudonyms.

*Authors' note:* The research reported here was supported by a grant to the authors (R305T010692-02) from the Office of Educational Research and Improvement, U.S. Department of Education. The opinions expressed here are those of the authors and are not necessarily endorsed by the U.S. Department of Education.

## References

Alexander, K. L., Entwisle, D. R., & Olson, L. S. (2007). Lasting consequences of the summer learning gap. *American Sociological Review, 72*(2), 167–180.

Allington, R. L., McGill-Franzen, A. M., Camilli, G., Williams, L., Graff, J., Zeig, J., et al. (2007, April). *Ameliorating summer reading setback among economically disadvantaged elementary students.* Paper presented at the American Educational Research Association Annual Meeting, Chicago.

Borman, G. D., Hewes, G. M., Overman, L. T., & Brown, S. (2003). Comprehensive school reform and achievement: A meta-analysis. *Review of Educational Research, 73*(1), 125–139.

Constantino, R. (2005). Print environments between high and low socioeconomic status communities. *Teacher Librarian, 32*(3), 22–25.

Cooper, H., Nye, B., Charlton, K., Lindsay, J., & Greathouse, S. (1996). The effects of summer vacation on achievement test scores: A narrative and meta-analytic review. *Review of Educational Research, 66*(2), 227–268.

Fryer, R. G., & Levitt, S. D. (2002). *Understanding the black-white test score gap in the first two years of school.* Cambridge, MA: National Bureau of Economic Research.

Hayes, D. P., & Grether, J. (1983). The school year and vacations: When do students learn? *Cornell Journal of Social Relations, 17*(1), 56–71.

Heyns, B. (1978). *Summer learning and the effects of schooling.* New York: Academic Press.

Kim, J. (2004). Summer reading and the ethnic achievement gap. *Journal of Education of Students at Risk, 9*(2), 169–189.

Kim, J. S. (2006). Effects of a voluntary summer reading intervention on reading achievement: Results from a randomized field trial. *Educational Evaluation and Policy Analysis, 28*(4), 335–355.

McQuillan, J., & Au, J. (2001). The effect of print access on reading frequency. *Reading Psychology, 22*(3), 225–248.

Neuman, S., & Celano, D. (2001). Access to print in low-income and middle-income communities. *Reading Research Quarterly, 36*(1), 8–26.

Neuman, S. B., Celano, D. C., Greco, A. N., & Shue, P. (2001). *Access for all: Closing the book gap for children in early education.* Newark, DE: International Reading Association.

**Anne McGill-Franzen** (amcgillf@utk.edu) and **Richard Allington** (rallingt@utk.edu) are Professors at the University of Tennessee, Knoxville.

Originally published in the April 2008 issue of *Educational Leadership, 65*(7): pp. 20–23.

# 12

# Teaching the 22 Percent

Teresa M. Burke

*A teacher from a high-poverty urban school*
*reflects on the choices she's made.*

After my school entered Program Improvement under No Child Left Behind, our union negotiated a provision that allowed teachers to transfer to a school of their choice that wasn't in Program Improvement. Even without that opportunity, teacher turnover at my high-poverty, urban school has long been problematic. I have worked with 20 different grade-level partners over 12 years, and we've had seven teachers in our three 5th grade classes in the last three years. I have been the only constant.

Those of us who choose to teach at high-poverty, urban schools have a variety of personal narratives that pull us back year after year. In my case, it was my dream as a teenager to become a teacher, which was thwarted early on and not pursued again until my 40s. It was also the ability, after 16 years of practicing law, to retire and take a more than 50 percent cut in pay. It was my father's suicide when he was 85, when I was his primary caregiver. It was the realization that I would never have children. These and a long list of other, smaller factors are what led me here.

## My Beliefs

Regardless of our specific narratives, those of us who teach in high-poverty schools often have a deep-rooted belief that we are working to create a better future for our children, our community, and our country. This belief often makes us flexible and open to new theories and strategies. It drives many of us to master today's technology and to yearn for a supportive team of like-minded people. We believe in children, knowing that our future is in their hands.

We believe in the immigrant child who writes a narrative titled "The Killing in Iraq" about events she witnessed firsthand. We believe in the undocumented immigrant student who struggles to learn English and says, "Teacher, I like this grammar stuff. It *really* makes sense!" We are kindred spirits with the father who proclaims at a conference, "My son is a good boy. He will make the United States of America proud."

Many of us who teach in these schools are white, middle-class women. According to the National Center for Education Statistics, 84 percent of public elementary school teachers are female, and 83 percent of full-time teachers are white.[1] I fit that stereotype, and I choose to be here each day. This is only one of the many choices within my reach.

## My Choices

I can choose to continually improve my teaching. I can choose to reach for stronger teaching strategies, more effective lesson ideas, and greater personalization of instruction. If a child is not making progress, I can choose to change what I'm doing, rather than find deficits with the student or the student's family. Many people have told me that if I want better results, I should change schools. But I like my school. I love my students. I do not want to leave. I want to be successful right where I am.

I choose to push my students. I want to bring them the kind of rigor I experienced in 16 years of Catholic school. I want to challenge their thinking, not fill them up with facts. I want to teach them to ask questions and analyze issues from every angle. My students are thinkers and problem solvers, as these stories attest:

- Early in the school year, the students file in talking loudly, bickering, complaining, ignoring all requests to quiet down and get busy. I chastise them and request silence—with no apparent result. A student looks at me and quietly says, "They don't trust you." I look back and say, "Yet." She smiles and says, "Yeah. Yet."
- A student drags out his, "What?" when being corrected for the third time, and I say, "How about if you try 'OK, no problem?'" Later that afternoon, as he looks to make sure no one else can hear, he asks me, "How am I doing on that OK stuff?"
- After a student is absent, he whispers quietly, "Can you please give me a minilesson on the math I missed? I really need to get caught up." I nod but make sure not to give him away in front of his friends.

My students are hungry for knowledge. They want to be confident with the right answer, and they want a taste of success. So I choose to focus on their skills and their desire to learn, and I choose to invest in a personal toolbox that will help me find ways to give them the success they crave.

## My Toolbox

All teachers assemble a personal toolbox of skills and strategies. Yet after working with 20 different teaching partners, I have come to believe that these personal toolboxes are insufficient. I am ineffective alone. I need a well-trained team of like-minded teachers who function cohesively and make continual learning a priority.

- *A well-trained team.* Each of us brings different strengths and skills to the table. Only when we combine these will we find lasting success in high-poverty, urban schools. Our culture, our communities, and our policies must make the education of *all* students a priority.
- *Like-minded teachers.* When teachers share similar philosophies and effectively collaborate with one another, students see that teamwork and harmony are realistic goals. It is crucial that we build a team of teachers who put aside individual needs and differences for the sake of the children. Teachers like me who also live in the community have an even greater investment in the success of the school and its students.
- *Cohesiveness.* Teachers need the time, the training, the desire, and a deep-rooted sense of unity and trust to function cohesively. We need to work collaboratively and willingly in an open and professional exchange of ideas, plans, efforts, and even failures.
- *Ability to continually learn.* We can equip ourselves with the knowledge, understanding, and worldview to ensure that we are as effective as possible, knowing that our personal narratives are very different from those of our students. We can pursue education in multicultural awareness and other areas that will expand our points of view and challenge us to reflect on our privilege and assumptions about social class, race, culture, and power.

We all have choices. With 22 percent of children in the United States living in poverty,[2] I am proud to be a 22 percent teacher. It is work that requires time and sacrifice. It is a choice within our reach.

# Endnotes

[1] National Center for Education Statistics. (2012). *The condition of education*. Washington, DC: U.S. Department of Education. Retrieved from http://nces.ed.gov/programs/coe/indicator_tsp.asp

[2] DeNavas-Walt, C., Proctor, B. D., & Smith, J. C. (2011). *Income, poverty, and health insurance coverage in the United States: 2010*. Washington, DC: U.S. Census Bureau. Retrieved from www.census.gov/prod/2011pubs/p60-239.pdf

**Teresa M. Burke** (tburke@sanjuan.edu) is a 5th grade teacher at Howe Avenue Elementary School in Sacramento, California.

Originally published online in the May 2013 issue of *Educational Leadership*, *70*(8).

# 13

# Teachers Who Stare Down Poverty

Carol Ann Tomlinson

*How teachers help students rewrite their prospects.*

My family wasn't wealthy when I was a kid, but neither did I experience mealtimes without food on the table, holidays without gifts, or sickness without resources to visit a doctor. Poverty existed only on the fringes of my world.

My first encounter with poverty that felt "real" came when some friends and I took toys and food to the house of a woman who worked in our college cafeteria. This woman, whom I'll call Mary, was cheerful and funny and paid attention to students in a way that made us feel seen. One day, when my friends and I drove by, we saw Mary at a bus stop crying. We stopped and asked if we could give her a ride. "I'm sorry you had to see me crying like that," she said. "I'm a single mom. Sometimes it seems too hard."

We didn't know what to do, but we wanted to help. So later we brought by things we thought Mary's kids would like. In her house were three little children asleep on two mattresses on a concrete floor. It was cold, and the smell was unfriendly. There were some clothes folded on a table (with no chairs) near a window that was too tall for the children to see out. I can still recall the physical feeling of fear that made me want to run away.

I wasn't afraid of the neighborhood and certainly not of Mary, who felt like a friend. But I wanted to escape what I instantly sensed to be a problem beyond my capacity to understand, let alone address.

## Learning Not to Run

I've thought of that moment often in my years as a teacher. In some small, important way, Mary sensitized me to the lives of students who came to my classroom from similar circumstances—and returned to those circumstances night after night. I understand the weight of their world better than I once did. Yet in some ways, I still have to fight the urge to turn away from the immensity of their challenges because I feel so inadequate to address their needs.

Over time, however, I've learned from children who live in poverty—and from educators who risk involvement with those children because to do otherwise is unthinkable to them. These educators are coarchitects and coengineers of possibility.

## The Architecture of a Dream

Certain beliefs and practices are central in the lives of educators who help children of poverty turn their hopes for better lives into reality. These educators

- Believe without reservation in the capacity of each student to succeed personally and academically. They accept as a given that there are few limits on what individuals can accomplish through hard, savvy work.

- See richness in the lives, experiences, and cultures of youth they mentor. They affirm the strengths that are an inevitable part of every young life.
- Connect on a level that conveys belief in a young person's worth. They persist in giving this message even when the youth rejects connection—often from fear that another adult will let him or her down.
- Make their faith in the young person visible by offering opportunities for new experiences to expand that child's sense of possibilities. Whether it's an offer to go to computer camp, a chance to join a group of kids going to a basketball game or a play, an invitation to study with others in the teacher's room during lunch, or a suggestion to try out for a team or a choir, the message is that the educator can imagine these students succeeding in a context they have considered closed to them—and will support the opportunity.
- Help the young person learn to set goals and take actions toward accomplishing them. Goal-setting and planning are learned skills crucial to success in almost any area. Educators who stare down poverty don't assume students come equipped with those skills.
- Take a diagnostic/prescriptive approach to developing students' academic skills. They determine which skills the student will need in order to pursue a goal and cultivate those skills. This may include helping with reading, writing, public speaking, applying for college, advocating for yourself in situations in which you feel wronged, using public transportation, or many other skills that students from privileged backgrounds assimilate.
- Support students in learning to live comfortably in two worlds. Often the invitation to build a dream is an invitation to move into a different circle of life, one remote from the familiar.

Teachers must help young people become bicultural. Rather than suggesting that kids from poverty backgrounds must leave behind language, music, customs, and other elements that shape their lives, these mentors help students extend their experiences while still valuing the experiences they grew up with—and deal with the accompanying emotional tensions.

- Build networks that support both achieving and belonging. It's lonely to have aspirations that set you apart from friends. Finding peers who have similar dreams or who have recently taken significant steps toward such dreams enhances the likelihood of persisting in the face of inevitable difficulty. Likewise, networks of caring adults throughout the school and community provide concrete evidence that there is support for this journey.
- Sign on for the long haul. Difficult roads are seldom either short or straight. These mentor-educators accept that the students whom they champion at age 10 will still need their support at 16. When failures happen, they help the student refocus, regroup, and restart.

Whether they become activists for social justice or quiet guides through a sort of "underground railroad," these educators help kids rewrite their prospects. We're all better for what they do—and for what we can learn to do from them.

---

**Carol Ann Tomlinson** (cat3y@virginia.edu) is William Clay Parrish Jr. Professor and Chair of Educational Leadership, Foundation, and Policy at the Curry School of Education, University of Virginia in Charlottesville. She is the author, with Marcia B. Imbeau, of *Leading and Managing a Differentiated Classroom* (ASCD, 2010).

Originally published in the May 2013 issue of *Educational Leadership*, 70(8): pp. 88–89.

# 14

# Tough Questions for Tough Times

William Parrett and Kathleen Budge

*In high-poverty schools, leaders can find the right answers to raising student achievement—when they start with the right questions.*

"It's cool to do well at Granger," exclaimed a 16-year-old we interviewed during a break in her daily advisory meeting. "It didn't used to be that way here, my sister told me ... but that's all different now. I'm hoping to go to the university in two years!"

Located in Washington State's rural Yakima Valley, Granger High School serves 388 mostly Hispanic students, 89 percent of whom qualify for free or reduced-price lunch. Over the past eight years, the school's 10th grade reading performance has steadily climbed from fewer than 20 percent of students meeting Washington state standards to nearly 80 percent. Parent attendance at student conferences has grown from a dismal 10 percent to almost 100 percent, and the graduation rate has soared to over 89 percent. As the staff's expectations of and relationships with students have grown, everything about the school has improved.

Two thousand miles to the east, in Saint Paul, Minnesota, 341 elementary students parade through the impoverished neighborhood surrounding Dayton's Bluff Elementary School. They're celebrating having accomplished their goal of reading a million words in the past year. "Twenty-five books read this year by each of our students, and we're letting our community know about it!" proudly proclaims Principal Andrew Collins, who leads the K–6 march with a bullhorn, while the students follow with noisemakers and banners.

Dayton's Bluff has risen from being the lowest-performing elementary school in Saint Paul—and one of the lowest-performing in Minnesota—to becoming a school in which nearly 70 percent of students meet or surpass state standards in reading and 75 percent meet or surpass state standards in math.

## From Low- to High-Performing

These schools demonstrate that it's possible not only to reverse historic trends of underachievement but also to sustain their gains. So how did they do it?

Leaders in schools like Granger and Dayton's Bluff began their remarkable turnarounds by making tough calls—and many of those decisions were about how to use resources. The budget in a high-performing, high-poverty school is a *moral document*, reflective of the school's beliefs about the conditions necessary to sustain success for all students and the adults who serve them. As budgets constrict, school leaders maintain their success by working collaboratively with staff to stay focused on the priorities that guide their work. They know that cuts in critical resources can jeopardize their hard-won gains. Countering these challenges becomes their top leadership priority.

On the basis of a growing body of knowledge that has emerged from the research on school effects (Teddlie & Stringfield, 1993), coupled with more recent analyses of strategies that have guided hundreds of schools in their successful efforts to reverse historic trends of underachievement (Barr & Parrett, 2006; Calkins, Guenther, Belfiore, &

Lash, 2007; Chenowith, 2007; Duke, 2007), we initiated a study seeking to understand how school leaders' actions influence a turnaround in low-performing schools.

In addition to Granger High and Dayton's Bluff, we visited four other high-performing/high-poverty schools: Taft Elementary in Boise, Idaho; P.S./M.S. 124, an elementary school in Queens, New York; Lapwai Elementary on the Nez Perce Reservation in northern Idaho; and Port Chester Middle School in Port Chester, New York. Despite high levels of poverty in their communities, these schools have sustained improvements on multiple measures of student success (achievement test scores, graduation rates, attendance rates, and behavior measures); and national and state organizations have recognized and honored them for their achievements.

An important message reverberates from these successes: A school can indeed overcome the powerful and pervasive effects of poverty on a student's learning. Sustained improvements usually began with an individual or a small group of leaders committed to equity and the goal of successfully teaching every student.

## Asking the Right Questions

The economic downturn and the recent passage of the American Recovery and Reinvestment Act confront many district and school leaders with the confounding paradox of managing both recession-driven budget cuts and new stimulus funding intended to improve the achievement of underserved students.

Leaders in high-performing/high-poverty schools begin by asking questions. The questions leaders ask fall into three interrelated domains: (1) building the necessary leadership capacity; (2) focusing the staff's everyday core work on student, professional, and system learning; and (3) creating and fostering a safe, healthy, and supportive learning environment for all. In tough times like these, their questions may provide valuable guidance for other school leaders facing their own challenges and opportunities.

## Questions About Leadership

*Do we have a data system that works for classroom and school leaders?*

All schools in the study have implemented data systems to guide their work. In fact, using data-based decision making was one of the two most common explanations offered for the schools' success. (The other was fostering caring relationships.)

Professional development in using data-based decision making, coupled with establishing measurable goals and developing aggressive time lines to achieve them, is vital to sustaining Lapwai Elementary's success. Concerned about the quality and level of teacher-parent communications, Lapwai staff members decided to set a schoolwide goal to have weekly contacts with families. They held themselves accountable by reporting their contacts to the principal, Teri Wagner, who shared the data at the district's board of trustees meetings.

*Are we eliminating policies and practices that manufacture low achievement?*

Research on the negative effects of low expectations, inequitable funding, retention, tracking, and mis-assignment to special education are well documented. All the schools studied confronted such policies and practices.

When Richard Esparza came to Granger High as principal 10 years ago, changing beliefs about students' potential was foundational to all the other actions he took. He began by modeling his belief in students' ability to meet high academic standards and by stating that he expected the faculty to believe the same thing. He worked with teachers to eliminate a bell-curve mentality—accepting that some students will fail—and a policy of one-chance testing. Instead, students who fall below a C in their coursework are now required to get extra help, and they can retake tests until they earn a C or better.

*Have we extended learning time for underachieving students?*

Underachieving students living in poverty require more instructional time to catch up to their higher-achieving peers. All high-performing/high-poverty schools find a way to extend learning time for students who need it. The schools offer a blend of before- and after-school tutoring, weekend and vacation catch-up sessions, summer school and full-day kindergarten, and sheltered classroom support. At Queens's P.S./M.S. 124, for example, school is in session "pretty much five and a half days per week," according to principal Valarie Lewis. On Saturday mornings, middle school students who need to catch up attend small learning academies.

*Have we reorganized time to better support professional learning?*

Eighty percent of a district's or school's budget is typically allocated toward personnel; becoming a high-performing school therefore requires making significant investments in people. Schools must find their own ways to reorganize time to support the development of communities of practice (Wenger, 1998). They can repurpose time traditionally set aside for faculty meetings, reorganize the schedule to accommodate common planning time, bank time for professional development, or locate funds for ongoing release time.

At Dayton's Bluff Elementary, grade-level teams of teachers use release time to review classroom-based assessment data, discuss instructional strategies, and plan for each upcoming six-week period. As teachers discuss individual students' performance and specific teaching strategies, the school's literacy coach and a district-level instructional coach look on and take part. By participating in collaborative planning sessions, coaches are better able to provide just-in-time support.

## Questions About Learning

*Does our instructional framework guide curriculum, teaching, assessment, and the learning climate?*

Leaders in the schools we studied credit much of their success to a high level of instructional program coherence. Several of the schools began their improvement efforts by adopting a comprehensive school reform model. For example, P.S./M.S. 124 selected Core Knowledge, whose framework emphasizes building students' knowledge base in world history, geography, civics, literature, science, art, and music.

Schools customized the reform models to better fit their needs. Finding the content to be "too Eurocentric," teachers at P.S./M.S. 124 have added content relating to Africa, Latin America, and Asia. In addition, they have incorporated knowledge about the various ethnicities and cultures represented in their student body.

*Do we have common assessments, and do we embrace assessment literacy?*

High-performing/high-poverty schools establish clear learning targets and engage their students in activities that help them acquire assessment literacy. These activities include selecting individual learning benchmarks, compiling portfolios, making public presentations of work, completing reflective revisions, and participating in student-led conferences.

Leaders in the Lapwai School District use professional learning time to focus on developing assessment literacy and common classroom-based assessments. At Granger High, the initiation of student-led conferences not only improved students' understanding of their own learning, but also significantly improved parents' attendance rates at their child's conferences.

*Are all students proficient in reading?*

Second only to safety, ensuring that all students develop literacy skills became a priority in most of the schools we studied. Designing a comprehensive approach to reading improvement may entail conducting an analysis of students' unique needs (for example, those of English language learners); developing an understanding of the influence of poverty on reading achievement (Neuman, 2008); and examining the research base, especially concerning adolescent literacy (see Slavin, Cheung, Groff, & Lake, 2008).

All teachers at Port Chester Middle School consider themselves to be English language arts teachers. To sell this idea, school leaders began by helping teachers understand that students' inability to read proficiently was a significant barrier to learning the content the teachers were attempting to teach. Now all teachers teach 24 bundled key reading and writing skills.

*Do we provide targeted interventions?*

The schools we studied use data to identify students who need before-, during-, and after-school small-group and individual tutoring; self-paced interventions using technology; one-on-one academic advising and coaching; homework support; or additional assessment time.

Taft Elementary in Idaho focuses on developing literacy skills early. The school offers full-day kindergarten and keeps class sizes small. In addition to the district-adopted reading program, Taft assesses the proficiency of all students and, if necessary, assigns students to one of three different reading interventions that provide different approaches to literacy learning.

## Questions About the Learning Environment

*Is our school safe?*

In all the schools studied, particularly the secondary schools, leaders emphasized safety for students and staff as a prerequisite for learning.

At Port Chester Middle School, principal Carmen Macchia explained, "In the beginning ... kids would hold their bladders all day out of fear of what might happen to them in the bathrooms." The school established structures, such as the frequent presence of school staff in bathrooms and hallways, to help students become accountable for their actions. The staff's expectations and modeling of appropriate behavior and other good citizenship practices encouraged students to help promote school safety, which authentically contributed to changing students' perspectives from one of "ratting out" their friends to one of civic responsibility to their school.

*Do we understand the influence of poverty on student learning?*

Although the concept of a culture of poverty has been refuted (Gorski, 2008), too many educators continue to believe that people who live in poverty share a common set of beliefs, values, attitudes, and behaviors (such as a poor work ethic, alcohol or drug abuse, and apathy toward school). To counter these myths, leaders in the schools we studied use data and research to support high expectations of students. An ethos of professional accountability for learning is tangible in all the participating schools, in contrast to schools that blame students and families for poor achievement.

When Taft Elementary School welcomed more than 60 refugee students one year from 16 different countries, principal Susan Williamson knew the importance of developing an understanding of the cultural and socioeconomic characteristics of the refugee students' families (Budge & Parrett, 2009). Enlisting the help of a former refugee whom the refugee community trusted, Susan and a small team of teacher leaders conducted multiple visits to each student's home. Although the purpose of these visits was to invite students to a two-week summer camp designed to familiarize the students with Taft and foster friendships, the visits also helped teachers gain a much better understanding of the cultural and socioeconomic influences on these students' lives.

*Have we fostered a bond between students and school?*

The high-performing/high-poverty schools we studied provided "protective factors" that help build a bond between students and school. Paramount among these factors is promoting caring relationships between adults and students as well as among peers.

Although Granger is a small high school serving only 388 students, many students felt disconnected from school. Former principal Esparza's focus on personalization led the staff to reorganize the school day to include a well-designed advisory program. All professional staff members, including the principal, advise a small group of 18–20 students four days each week and stay with those students for four years, navigating their path toward graduation and beyond. The advisory teacher regularly reviews each student's progress through school-generated biweekly reports, holding students accountable for staying on track. Advisors identify any student who falls behind and work with the student's teachers to intervene. "It's all about relationships with the kids," explained current principal Paul Chartrand, "and the advisory program is key to our continued success."

Other high-performing/high-poverty schools provide additional protective factors, such as restructuring into small learning communities and removing economic barriers to participation in various extracurricular activities. Some schools work to counter the adverse effects of student mobility by dedicating staff to the task of welcoming and placing new students.

*Do we engage parents, families, and the community?*

High-performing/high-poverty schools do not go it alone. Instead, they build positive and productive relationships with students' families and the broader neighborhood and community. In partnership with the city of Saint Paul and the Amherst H. Wilder Foundation, Dayton's Bluff Elementary provides students and families with a recreational facility and the services of a nurse-practitioner, dentist, and social worker at the school.

Leaders in the schools we studied engage stakeholders in various ways—for example, hiring a school/family/community liaison, offering adult mentoring and community service learning programs, ensuring two-way communication between the school and the family, and using the school as a community center.

## Tough Decisions, Tough Times

Leaders in the six schools we studied expressed confidence that the processes they had in place would guide their decisions regarding the use of possible stimulus funding. The principals voiced concern for two top priorities: (1) maintaining and perhaps adding staff, because keeping personnel is key to a low student-teacher ratio and caring relationships in school; and (2) providing targeted support to the students who need it most. "Target the lowest-performing kids," cautioned one principal, "even if the stimulus money doesn't last forever."

Leaders in high-performing/high-poverty schools recognize their efforts and successes as a continuing journey. Whether surviving budget cuts, carefully targeting new stimulus funding, or both, leaders in all schools may benefit from reflecting on the questions leaders ask in high-performing/high-poverty schools to support and sustain student success.

## References

Barr, R., & Parrett, W. (2006). *The kids left behind.* Bloomington, IN: Solution Tree.

Budge, K., & Parrett, W. (2009). Making refugee students welcome [Online article.]. *Educational Leadership, 66*(7). Available at www.ascd.org/publications/educational_leadership/apr09/num07/Making_Refugee_Students_Welcome.aspx.

Calkins, A., Guenther, W., Belfiore, G., & Lash, D. (2007). *The turn-around challenge: Why America's best opportunity to dramatically improve student achievement lies in our worst-performing schools.* Boston: Mass Insight Education and Research Institute.

Chenowith, K. (2007). *"It's being done": Academic successes in unexpected schools*. Cambridge, MA: Harvard University Press.

Duke, D. (2007, February 21). Turning schools around. *Education Week, 26*(24), 35–37.

Gorski, P. (2008). The myth of the culture of poverty. *Educational Leadership, 65*(7), 32–36.

Neuman, S. (2008). The mediating mechanisms of the effects of poverty on reading achievement. In S. Neuman (Ed.), *Educating the other America: Top experts tackle poverty, literacy, and achievement in our schools.* (pp. 1–16). Baltimore: Brooks Publishing.

Slavin, R., Cheung, A., Groff, C., & Lake, C., (2008). Effective reading programs for middle and high schools: A best-evidence synthesis. *Reading Research Quarterly, 43*(3), 290–322.

Teddlie, C., & Stringfield, S. (1993). *Schools make a difference: Lessons learned from a ten-year study of school effects.* New York: Teachers College Press.

Wenger, E. (1998). *Communities of practice: Learning, meaning, and identity.* New York: Cambridge University Press.

**William Parrett** (wparret@boisestate.edu) is Director of the Center for School Improvement and Policy Studies and **Kathleen Budge** (kathleenbudge@boisestate.edu) is Coordinator of the Educational Leadership program at Boise State University in Idaho. They are the authors of *Turning High-Poverty Schools into High-Performing Schools* (ASCD, 2012).

Originally published in the October 2009 issue of *Educational Leadership, 67*(2): pp. 22–27.

# 15

# Making a Difference Every Day: A Conversation with Salome Thomas-EL

Naomi Thiers

*A Philadelphia principal talks about how to
develop relationships with children.*

Salome Thomas-EL has spent his life making a difference for kids in high-poverty schools in Philadelphia, as a teacher and principal. He inspires students through chess (the Vaux Middle School chess teams he coached were eight-time National Chess Champions) and through his own story: Raised by a single mother in Philadelphia's housing projects, he became an award-winning educator. He is author of *I Choose to Stay: A Black Teacher Refuses to Desert the Inner City* (Kensington, 2003) and *The Immortality of Influence* (Kensington, 2010) and is a regular contributor on The Dr. Oz Show.

**You've said you still hear the voices of teachers who encouraged you. Do you think teachers have a unique influence on how young people see their life possibilities?**

I do. I often say teachers are "saving Private Ryan" every day. I see students in the schools where I work who hang on every word a teacher says. That influence is so powerful because for many students, that teacher becomes their mother, their father, their counselor, their nutritionist, their life coach.

Many young people are the first in their families to have an opportunity to get a college education. It's very powerful for a teacher to be open with a young person and say, "I made mistakes. I lived a tough life, but look where I am now. You can grow up and become even more than I am." Just living your life in such a way that students understand when you say, "You can be me because I was once you."

**You grew up in tough circumstances. What did teachers say or do for you that helped you believe you could achieve whatever you wanted to?**

It might have been more about what teachers *didn't* say to me. I don't remember many teachers allowing me to believe that I was gifted or that I had reached my potential. We're learning so much now about the growth mind-set and fixed mind-set, but 40 years ago, teachers I had in elementary, middle, and high school knew that if young people didn't understand that failure was part of becoming successful, they would become complacent.

I would often complain to my mother, "These teachers, they just push me, like I can never make them happy." Now I understand what it was: They wanted me to avoid that fixed mind-set.

Powerful educators like Marsha Pincus—my high school English teacher—and others taught me that I could make a difference. Marsha Pincus taught me to love Shakespeare and Chaucer. When she went out on maternity leave, the substitute was trying to teach a lesson on literature, and the students were giving the sub a tough time. So I said, "Can I help teach the lesson?" I loved literature so much that I wanted the teacher to get through this lesson.

I wrote Marsha Pincus a letter from college and told her that I'd enrolled in an advanced literature course. None of my friends wanted to take this course, but I was thinking Ms. Pincus would be upset with me if I didn't take it. She told me later that she kept that letter because up until that point, she never thought she was a good teacher. She was a young white teacher in a high school in a tough neighborhood who didn't really know if she was making a difference.

I'm the only one of my mother's eight children to graduate from college. Teachers would ask me why some of my older brothers and sisters weren't as successful in school. They'd say, "You have the ability to go on and do things in life and come back and make sure other families don't end up in the same situation."

I didn't realize it, but that was a call to become a teacher. My goal was to become a sportscaster, but getting that call to become a teacher was the most important moment in my life. Even in college, when I talked about wanting to be an attorney, a professor showed me data on the number of lawyers in the country. He said, "I want you to make a difference; think about becoming a teacher."

After I graduated from college, I was working for a sports cable channel. I went to a school to talk to students at career day, and they said to me," If you can come in and motivate us, how come you aren't a teacher?" Those young people were teaching me that I had become the kind of person that I complained about—someone who made it out of the community, was successful, but didn't come back to do anything to help change the community.

So I quit my TV job and got a certificate to teach. I spent the next 10 years working in a middle school in a very tough neighborhood. We lost almost 20 kids under the age of 18 to murder, many of them from our school. I said to myself, I've got to find a way to teach children that although they can choose the behavior, they cannot choose the consequences. That's why I started teaching students to play chess.

**What skills do students get from learning chess? Is chess particularly helpful for kids from poor, urban neighborhoods?**

Students who play chess are critical thinkers, problem solvers. It teaches you to think two, three, four moves ahead. Chess gives students the ability to make great decisions at crucial moments. A child who lives in a tough neighborhood has to make life-changing decisions every day in terms of what they do. They must always be aware of the friends they associate with or what streets to walk down at night, for example.

Learning chess can also give students intellectual capital. The students I taught to play chess started beating me, started beating the other teachers, and then all the kids wanted to play chess. They learned that smart is not something you are; it's something you can become.

Chess is very mathematical. In my first teaching job, with middle school students, I started using chess to teach mathematics. Now I have 2nd, 3rd, and 4th graders writing their chess moves in algebraic notation. Those children are very good thinkers. If we want to be innovative, we need to make sure there's a chess program in every school in the world.

**You've said discipline was the most important thing you taught. How can we provide discipline that makes a difference?**

Discipline is a form of love. There are ways to discipline children with dignity that enable them to still feel good about themselves, to continue to be proud of their accomplishments, but also to understand that they've made a mistake and need to take responsibility.

Some students are not accustomed to discipline, so when you discipline them, they feel that's not the norm. Their reactions can be violent or disrespectful. But that's the only thing they know; their reaction is a normal reaction to an abnormal situation. We have to be careful about how we deliver discipline because they may not be ready for it.

Once I had a student in my office with his mother. He was giving teachers problems, didn't want to do homework and those kinds of things. Clearly, he didn't show much respect in the way he was treating his mom, the way he was talking to her. I asked his mother if I could talk to the young man by himself.

I talked to him about my own life growing up with a single mom and how sometimes we can forget how lucky we are to have people in our lives. We get upset about the people who are *not* there. I could see this boy was upset that his father wasn't there for him—and later he confirmed that. I told him, "Think about the people who *are* there for you."

This was a kid who would play basketball with me and other teachers in the evening. If we had events on the weekend, we would invite him and help him get there. So I said, "I don't think it's fair that you treat your mom in that way and then we take you to these events and give you special treatment. Your parent is very important."

He was homeless, so I had to be very careful and loving about the way I presented it to him. But I knew this was going to be one of my only shots to send a message to this young man, because if it's his mom today, would it be his college professor soon, or someone who says, "Hey, you're going to lose your scholarship"? I didn't want him to become an adult—a professional—and then lose whatever he had because of the way he treated people.

And the young man responded to the call to be a better person. He became more respectful in school and at home. His mother saw tremendous change, even in the way he helped out with the family, being the oldest. He sort of became the father who wasn't there.

Many young people are being raised in an environment where there isn't structure. Students want structure, they want guidance, and they want you to be firm with them. They just don't know how to reach out for it. And they don't want the other young people to know they enjoy structure. Students never complain to me about the fact that there's too much structure in a class, but they'll come and say, "Oh, Principal, that class is out of control."

**You're called a "turnaround principal" at Thomas Edison Charter School. What can a principal do to make a difference in a troubled school?**

If you want to move a school in a different direction, first you have to change the culture of the school. And to change the culture, you have to be willing to accept the role as the prime facilitator of school culture. That means the relationships that you want teachers to develop with students need to be reflected in the relationships you develop with teachers. Treat those teachers with respect. Give them a leadership role in the school.

Second, the principal has to be passionate about his or her work and be able to ignite the building with excitement around education. And to make school fun. Two things you want students to experience every day in school are rigor and joy.

Third, administrators have to be excellent models of leadership. That's why I cover classes. When my math teacher went to Kuwait for two weeks, I taught the class. Those students could see that I valued their learning so much that I would spend time with them every day until that teacher returned.

Principals have to be smart enough to know that the people who are in the school are the exact people you need to get the job done. You don't need to go outside and look for experts; most schools have right within the building the people they need. When I go into a school to turn it around, I don't get rid of everybody because we have to respect the history in the school. We have to respect the legacy.

My mother taught me that arrogance is the Achilles heel of the school leader. She told me, if you want to be a successful principal, make sure you listen to the old ladies in the building, those teachers who've been there for principal after principal. They're teaching the children of the children they taught, and they know what it takes for schools to be successful. That has worked for me for 15 years!

It's important for students to be in a school where teachers are resilient. We often talk about resilient students, but we also need resilient teachers who are able to overcome obstacles early in their careers because many of their students will depend on them to be there for them, some of them for a lifetime.

I had a teacher in my office crying today because she got a phone call from a tough parent. I was trying to get the teacher to understand that the parent's frustration was about not finding successful ways to help her own child. But many times parents communicate that in a way that blames the teacher. Once the teacher understood where the parent's defensiveness was coming from, she could see it wasn't really about her ability as a teacher. It was about needing to find a way to help the parent as well.

**You've sometimes given students material help. For instance, when a student's house burned down, you collected money so her family could stay in a hotel. What is the school's role when students face material deprivation?**

The school belongs to the community. So whenever there's a family in need—whether there's a fire in the home or the family is homeless—the school has some responsibility. I'm very careful to say *some* responsibility because I don't want schools to think it's their job to take care of families. And I don't want families to believe it's the school's responsibility to do that; I don't want parents to move away from caring for their children. I've seen examples where the school offered so much support that we began to see family caregivers back away. We want to support families to support their children. But I believe we have a responsibility as citizens, as educators, to make sure that students' basic needs are met so they can come to school and be successful.

That young lady whose family I helped when their house burned down still contacts me today. She's graduated from college, she's a professional, and we have a bond because at a crucial point in her family's life, I took any resources I could find to help her family.

We must make sure that we're helping to develop the whole child. Academically things may be great, but what's going on outside school? What are your needs, and how can we connect you to services to help you become better equipped to succeed?

**Students in difficult circumstances sometimes won't ask for help, or will even resist it. How can teachers reach out if a student seems resistant?**

Many young people are very guarded about their emotions. They don't let you in right away. Many of them opened up to adults when they were younger, and the adults either took advantage of them emotionally or physically or just weren't there. So many young people have adults that come in and out of their lives that the teacher is the only person who's caring and offering healthy love—notice I said *healthy* love—consistently.

I tell teachers that persistence overcomes resistance. They'll complain that they're having a hard time getting to know a kid. I'll say, keep trying the key; one day you'll have the right key. Don't give up. I often suggest that teachers go to the neighborhood playground or the Laundromat—go to where those students are comfortable in their own communities. If it's not safe for them to go alone, I'll go with them. Students will often say, "Man, last night Principal Thomas-EL did a drive-by!"

As we keep persisting, there's a reverse influence in which students influence *us* in a very powerful way. They teach us to have humility; they teach us to really teach with care and passion and love because they choose to be with us. They make the choice to be under our influence.

**What's the most important thing a teacher can do to convince a child, "I believe in you."**

That's the crucial question every teacher will have to address at some point. The first thing a teacher must do is develop a relationship with that child so he or she understands that you will be there for him—no matter what, you'll be there tomorrow. That's why teacher retention is so important. Successful schools have teachers who are there every year, principals who are there every year. That doesn't mean 35 or 40 years, but you need to be there more than a year or two for young people to know that you will be part of their lives.

Make sure the student you're trying to reach has meaningful participation in school. Students need to feel they matter in the classroom. You can't allow a kid to hide. Even if you think he's going to answer the question wrong, still ask the question because struggling is learning.

Teachers need to share with students about their own lives. Many young people have this belief that teachers are born on some other planet, that we came down on a spaceship and never had to deal with any struggles. Children need to know that we're human beings and we have feelings. When they look at us, they should see themselves.

I have white teachers who will say, "How do I get a black kid or a Latino kid to understand that although I may not look like them, I'm here for them?" I say, "The only thing you need to do is tell that student, 'I will be here tomorrow—and although I may look different, my heart is the same and my heart is here to teach you.'"

Finally, it's more important for students to respect you than to like you. We all want students to like us, but students can like you and not do the work you assign. You want students to like being in your presence, but you should never sacrifice respect. It's difficult to teach anyone anything if they don't respect you or don't love you. I tell my teachers to adopt the philosophy that they love their students before they ever meet them. When you care about someone, you can teach them anything.

---

**Salome Thomas-EL** (http://principalel.com/) is principal of Thomas Edison Charter School in Wilmington, Delaware. **Naomi Thiers** is an associate editor at *Educational Leadership*.

Originally published in the June 2014 issue of *Educational Leadership*, *71*, pp. 10–15.

# Study Guide for
## *On Poverty and Learning:*
## *Readings from* Educational Leadership

Naomi Thiers and Teresa Preston

*Ideas to try out individually or in a study group.*

Students who live with poverty often come to school with problems that affect how well they learn. Despite caring about these students, teachers may feel ill-equipped to give these students the help they most need. How can teachers support these students so that they can find a path out of poverty and what role might schools have in giving students an equal chance at success, despite their unequal beginnings?

*EL* authors have tackled these questions from a variety of angles, looking at systemic problems that go beyond schools and offering suggestions for what classroom teachers might do.

## Whose Problem Is It?

Richard Rothstein ("Whose Problem is Poverty?") asserts that when we focus solely on school reforms as the cure for the achievement gap, we suppress discussion—and even awareness—of how the physical and social deprivations of poverty limit achievement. He notes:

> Teachers see for themselves how poor health or family eco-
> nomic stress impedes students' learning. Teachers may nowa-
> days be intimidated from acknowledging these realities aloud
> and may, in groupthink obedience, repeat the mantra that "all
> children can learn." But nobody is fooled. Teachers still know
> that although all children can learn, some learn less well be-
> cause of poorer health or less-secure homes. (p. 42)

- Discuss a time when you observed that a student's stress-
  ful home conditions (from poverty or some other source)
  impeded his or her learning. Were you able to make up for
  these conditions by redoubling your efforts at good instruction targeted toward this student's needs?
- When you have taught students from impoverished families,
  did inadequate health care, frequent moves, or lack of adult
  attention make achievement more difficult? Describe what
  you observed and how you responded.
- Do you think closing the achievement gap is within teachers'
  and administrators' control—or is this a myth, as Rothstein
  believes? If you believe that educators *can't* completely
  close the gap even through stellar practice, what keeps you
  striving to do your best?

## A Place for Ability Grouping?

Halley Potter ("Boosting Achievement by Pursuing Diversity") writes about the benefits of creating socioeconomically diverse schools. Read her discussion of whether ability grouping has a place in such schools and her examples of how some successfully integrated schools tackle the issue of differentiating instruction without resorting to resegregat-ing students through rigid ability grouping.

- What is your opinion of ability grouping in schools? Do the benefits of clustering students by ability level outweigh its disadvantages (diluting diversity and possibly keeping students stuck in low-level work)?
- What kind of ability grouping does your school or department engage in? How does it affect students? If you've been teaching more than 10 years, have you seen the tendency to group students by ability change over the years?
- Talk about the issue that Potter raises of encouraging students from different backgrounds or races to interact together socially. In your school, do students tend to self-segregate at lunchtime or to socialize? If so, has your school tried anything to break down this tendency? (Your group may want to consider reading sections of Beverly Daniel Tatum's 2003 book, *Why Are All the Black Kids Sitting Together in the Cafeteria?*).

## Rising Segregation—and its Consequences

Several articles discuss the reality that neighborhoods and schools across the United States are increasingly segregated by both race and income. "Students without money," writes Susan B. Neuman in "The American Dream: Slipping Away?", "are increasingly confined to homogeneously poor neighborhoods, yielding a density of material deprivation that is unprecedented in our history."

The stakes of segregation by income are high: Research shows that students from impoverished families tend to fare worse academically in high-poverty schools and better in schools with economically mixed student bodies.

Kids who grow up in neighborhoods with a high concentration of poverty are set back as readers, Neuman argues. Their environment offers fewer books, less enriching literacy work in school, and may even lack street signs that help develop the sight-to-sound connection.

Neuman and a colleague researched in detail the amount of literacy-related resources—from street signs free of graffiti to interactions with adults in the public library—available to children in one wealthy and one poor neighborhood in Philadelphia. Disparities were striking: the rich neighborhood boasted far more stores selling children's books, a wider selection of books within schools, more libraries, and so on.

- Does the pattern Neuman found bear up in your area? Think of a wealthy neighborhood and a poor one within a 30-minute drive of your school. Pooling your group's knowledge, do a rough estimate of how many bookstores (or stores that sell educational toys or kids' books) exist in each area. What's each library—especially the children's area—like (how big, how accessible, and in what sort of condition)?
- Take a short walk or drive through both communities; note how much inviting print (street signs, attractive store signs, and so on) you see in each. Observe for a brief time each area's public library; what do you notice?
- Consider Neuman's suggestions for "changing the trajectory" of how a lack of resources weakens the reading skills of poor children. Particularly if your school serves kids who live in neighborhoods similar to the Badlands, how might you carry out these suggestions in your school? Can you identify one change you could implement throughout the coming school year?
- Discuss Neuman's argument that to really change things, we must "un-level the playing field" by proving *more* resources and supports to kids in poor neighborhoods. Do you agree?
- For more perspectives, look at the special section on resegregation, featuring Jonathan Kozol, Beverly Daniel Tatum, and other leading voices, in the November 2010 *Educational Leadership*.

# Small Changes with Big Benefits

The task of creating equal education opportunities in a society full of uneven opportunities can seem nearly impossible. But, as Richard E. Nisbett reminds us in "Think Big, Bigger … and Smaller," even small changes can yield long-term benefits for students who start out at a disadvantage.

Consider one of the low-tech interventions Nisbett describes that has been shown to improve the school achievement of struggling students. When teachers clearly tell students about the powerful role that effort—as opposed to purely natural intelligence—plays in getting high grades, and show students that they themselves can build stronger neural connections through applying themselves to learning, even chronically failing students start to work harder and do better.

- Tune in to the messages that your school communicates to kids. Examine the language used to recognize high academic achievers, descriptions of famous people in textbooks and class readings, or even the comments you write on student work—about what leads to accomplishments: native ability or hard work? What might give students the message that only people with special abilities can achieve? How might you infuse messages about the importance of strong effort in a way that would motivate students who are far behind and discouraged?
- Spend a class or two talking with students about how the brain develops and how, through applying effort, they can actually strengthen their own intelligence (You may find the December 2009/January 2010 *EL* article "How to Teach Students about the Brain" and the accompanying downloadable handout for students helpful). Are your students aware that intelligence is malleable, or do they perceive it as a fixed commodity they either possess or don't? What about the low achievers in your class?

## Answering the Tough Questions

In "Tough Questions for Tough Times," William Parrett and Kathleen Budge explain how high-poverty schools have raised student achievement by closely examining their policies and practices.

- According to Parrett and Budge, a school's budget is "a moral document" that reveals what the school believes is necessary for student success. Do you agree with this statement? How can your school spend money more wisely?
- Parrett and Budge provide several questions about leadership, learning, and the learning environment for school leaders to think about. Choose one question from each category and examine how your school stacks up. What are you doing well, and how might you improve?
- Select one of Parrett and Budge's questions for more focused study. Gather data that helps answer the question, analyze the data, and develop a list of strategies for improvement.

**Naomi Thiers** is Associate Editor, *Educational Leadership*. **Teresa Preston** is a former Associate Editor of *Educational Leadership*.

# *EL Takeaways*
## On Poverty and Learning

"Students' socioeconomic backgrounds have a huge effect on their academic outcomes. But so do the backgrounds of the peers who surround them. Poor students in mixed-income schools do better than poor students in high-poverty schools." —*Halley Potter*

"They say, "Can you really solve this kind of problem by throwing money at it?" Conservatives love that word *throwing*. They never speak of throwing money at the Pentagon. We allocate money for the Pentagon. We throw money at anything that has to do with human pain." —*Jonathan Kozol*

"Learn every student's name. Ask about their family, their hobbies, and what's important to them. Stop telling students what to do and start teaching them how to do it." —*Eric Jensen*

"We need to tip the balance not by equalizing funding but by providing more resources and additional supports to students in poor neighborhoods. Not just extra funding, but additional human resources are needed." —*Susan B. Neuman*

"It's important for students to be in a school where teachers are resilient. We often talk about resilient students, but we also need resilient teachers who are able to overcome obstacles early in their careers because many of their students will depend on them to be there for them, some of them for a lifetime." —*Salome Thomas-EL*

"Being homeless does not mean being hopeless." —*Vicki S. Dill*

# Related ASCD Resources

At the time of publication, the following ASCD resources were available (ASCD stock numbers appear in parentheses). For up-to-date information about ASCD resources, go to www.ascd.org. You can search the complete archives of *Educational Leadership* at http://www.ascd.org/el.

**ASCD EDge®**
Exchange ideas and connect with other educators interested in math on the social networking site ASCD EDge at http://ascdedge.ascd.org.

**Print Products**

*Hanging In: Strategies for Teaching the Students Who Challenge Us Most* by Jeffrey Benson (#114013)

*Excellence Through Equity: Five Principles of Courageous Leadership to Guide Achievement for Every Student* by Alan M. Blankstein and Pedro Noguera with Lorena Kelly (#116070)

*Creating the Opportunity to Learn: Moving from Research to Practice to Close the Achievement Gap* by A. Wade Boykin & Pedro Noguera (#107016)

*Meeting Students Where They Live: Motivation in Urban Schools* by Richard L. Curwin (#109110)

*Engaging Students with Poverty in Mind: Practical Strategies for Raising Achievement* by Eric Jensen (#113001)

*Teaching with Poverty in Mind: What Being Poor Does to Kids' Brains and What Schools Can Do About It* by Eric Jensen (#109074)

*Turning High-Poverty Schools into High-Performing Schools* by William H. Parrett & Kathleen M. Budge (#109003)

*Fostering Resilient Learners: Strategies for Creating a Trauma-Sensitive Classroom* by Kristin Souers with Pete Hall (#116014)

**PD Online® Courses**
Teaching with Poverty in Mind (#PD11OC139M)

For more information: send e-mail to member@ascd.org; call 1-800-933-2723 or 703-578-9600, press 2; send a fax to 703-575-5400; or write to Information Services, ASCD, 1703 N. Beauregard St., Alexandria, VA 22311-1714 USA.

# WHOLE CHILD
# TENETS

## 1. HEALTHY
Each student enters school healthy and learns about and practices a healthy lifestyle.

## 2. SAFE
Each student learns in an environment that is physically and emotionally safe for students and adults.

## 3. ENGAGED
Each student is actively engaged in learning and is connected to the school and broader community.

## 4. SUPPORTED
Each student has access to personalized learning and is supported by qualified, caring adults.

## 5. CHALLENGED
Each student is challenged academically and prepared for success in college or further study and for employment and participation in a global environment.

ASCD's Whole Child approach is an effort to transition from a focus on narrowly defined academic achievement to one that promotes the long-term development and success of all children. Through this approach, ASCD supports educators, families, community members, and policymakers as they move from a vision about educating the whole child to sustainable, collaborative actions.

*On Poverty and Learning: Readings from* **Educational Leadership** relates to all five whole child tenets.

For more about the Whole Child approach, visit **www.wholechildeducation.org**.

LEARN. TEACH. LEAD.

CPSIA information can be obtained
at www.ICGtesting.com
Printed in the USA
BVHW030109270822
645671BV00012B/219